VINCENZO VENEZIA

anxiety in relationships

Essential Guide to Move Beyond Negative Thinking, Jealousy and Fear of Abandonment

Contents

INTRODUCTION — 1

CHAPTER 1: EIGHT SIGNS OF ANXIETY IN YOUR RELATIONSHIP — 7

1. CHAPTER 2: UNDERSTANDING THE ROOTS OF ANXIETY — 13

2. CHAPTER 3: HOW DO ATTACHMENT STYLES AFFECT YOUR LIFE? — 27

3. CHAPTER 4: EMPTY THE NEGATIVE THOUGHTS! — 43

4. CHAPTER 5: FEAR OF ABANDONMENT: OVERVIEW, SYMPTOMS, AND TREATMENT — 52

5. CHAPTER 6: BREAK FREE FROM JEALOUSY — 63

6. CHAPTER 7: TEN EARLY SIGNS OF A TOXIC RELATIONSHIP — 72

7. CHAPTER 8: BOOST YOUR SELF-ESTEEM 83

8. CHAPTER 9: NATURAL REMEDIES FOR ANXIETY RELIEF AND MANAGEMENT 98

9. CHAPTER 10: ANTI-ANXIETY EXERCISES 107

10. CHAPTER 11: COUPLES EXERCISES 114

11. CHAPTER 12: COMMON RELATIONSHIP MISTAKES 127

12. CHAPTER 13: RESTORATIVE PRACTICES TO RESOLVE CONFLICT 134

CHAPTER 14: COMMUNICATE BETTER WITH YOUR PARTNER 142

13. CHAPTER 15: LOVING A PERSON WITH ANXIETY 148

14. CHAPTER 16: TEN SURPRISING KEYS TO BUILDING A HEALTHY RELATIONSHIP 154

CONCLUSION 162

INTRODUCTION

Many readers may be shocked to find how widespread anxiety is. According to some estimates, anxiety disorders are thought to affect up to 30% of the general population at some point in their lives. Anxious symptoms will affect men and women worldwide, with millions of people likely to be affected by anxiety in any given year. Anxiety is thought to affect women roughly twice as often as males; also, nervousness is believed to be more common among adults in their mid-20s and older, making anxiety a key area of concern in the working-age population. Another startling fact about anxiety is that it appears to be more prevalent in Europe and the United States than in other regions.

When anxiety symptoms go untreated, they can cause major impairments in daily functioning, poor quality of life, and a large economic burden. In addition, anxiety disorders are especially relevant in the context of recent and current global conflicts, as environmental factors can significantly impact the development of anxiety and stress disorders, notably post-traumatic stress disorder (PTSD). Given the high incidence rates, harmful impacts on many aspects of functioning, and environmental factors linked with trauma and stress, we must continue to enhance our understanding of the mechanisms behind anxiety disorders in order to improve existing therapies.

Even though anxiety disorders have been extensively examined, the literature exploring underlying brain pathways remains limited, with scant evidence establishing unique abnormalities for various anxiety disorders. Despite a lack of detailed knowledge about the mechanisms behind anxiety, pharmaceutical (selective serotonin reuptake inhibitors) and psychotherapy (cognitive behavioral therapy) therapies for anxiety have been created. Although these treatments are useful for many patients, their precise mechanisms of action are unknown. Moreover, several patients do not have access to or achieve complete symptom alleviation from existing evidence-based treatments. As a result, we must continue to strive to better understand the precise neurological impairments underpinning anxiety disorders and the methods by which effective treatments diminish symptoms.

Anxiety disorders are generally classified based primarily on behavioral and subjective experiences. However, the brain pathways underpinning anxiety symptomatology may overlap across several illnesses. Indeed, some argue that anxiety disorders may exist on a spectrum ranging from specific fear-based reactions to more widespread and protracted worry or apprehension.

In truth, anxiety is an umbrella term for various disorders that can cause people to feel fearful or panicked. Although these illnesses are diverse, many of them are related to a certain fear pathway in the brain that some scientists believe indicates the human experience of worry. Karl Deisseroth, associate professor of psychiatry, behavioral sciences, and bioengineering, led a study team that identified two important pathways in the brain: one that promotes anxiety and the other that alleviates worry. These pathways are located in the amygdala, a brain area.

As social beings, humans engage in interactive communication when they enter a social setting, such as relationships with friends, relationships with family, or relationships with a partner. Despite the fact that most people have become accustomed to entering such social surroundings, many of them experience anxiety in circumstances such as completing an important test, singing a song in front of others, or interviewing for a job. These circumstances may result in bodily symptoms such as a racing heart, hot and shaky hands, and a parched mouth.

The extreme fear of being embarrassed and/or rejected by others is referred to as social anxiety. Individuals benefit from expressing their emotions and thoughts, and concealing sentiments or opinions can be detrimental to their mental health. Socially anxious people prefer to avoid their feelings as a safety strategy to prevent displaying negative emotions to others, as they believe doing so will lead to social blunders, shame, and rejection. These people are likely to be concerned about the negative effects of openly expressing emotions such as anxiousness and wrath toward another person.

After all, these emotional reactions may cause people to perceive them as undesirable or fragile, which can wreak havoc on their relationships. Socially apprehensive people are more likely to be socially isolated, or have unsatisfactory social relationships.

Another component contributing to relationship pleasure is attachment type. The notion of attachment considers the worth and power of the bond built between children and their parents, how this relationship is developed, and how the quality of this relationship might affect children's healthy development. According to attachment theory, people form cognitive structures, or working models, that symbolize their ability to rely on key persons in their lives. These working models are believed to play an important influence in molding people's relationship experiences. Subjects who have more secure attachments have higher levels of social support and lower levels of depression. Furthermore, several studies have revealed that stable attachment styles are associated with desirable outcomes such as life satisfaction, social efficacy, career exploration, and high subjective well-being.

Several researchers have found a link between attachment style and well-being. For example, researchers discovered that anxious attachment and well-being were inversely related and that this was more evident in the younger age group than in the older age. The outcomes of another study found that the avoidance dimension of attachment predicted people's life happiness. Therefore, it can be observed that attachment style and well-being significantly impact people's personal and social lives.

Furthermore, attachment style influences people's happiness in romantic relationships, life satisfaction, and subjective well-being. People with different attachment styles have varying views and feelings about their connection, love, the trustworthiness of their love partners, and their love worthiness. People acquire diverse perspectives about themselves from their social surroundings as a result of their attachment type.

Subjective well-being is another important part of relating that influences people's social experiences. Well-being indicates the extent to which people feel good about themselves and their life.

Being in a social setting and interacting with others are essential variables influencing people's lives and subjective well-being. Furthermore, the quality of people's lives is dictated by their relationships with others, such as friends, family members, or coworkers. Individuals regard their connection as desirable when they believe they can readily express their demands and emotions in their relationship or when they believe they can explain their thoughts whenever they want. Furthermore, when people speak with one another without inhibition or fear of being rejected and/or embarrassed, they can truly act like themselves.

When people introduce themselves in a relationship, they may discover that they have similar thoughts, personality traits, hobbies, and so on to their potential partner or friend. It is worth noting that various studies have found that greater similarity is related to higher levels of pleasure. Socially anxious persons often avoid self-introduction, are unable to discover common ground in relationships, and, as a result, are unable to be happy.

Humans must communicate with others from the moment they are born by entering a social setting. Therefore, individuals' success in life is tied to their ability to interact with their social surroundings, because people's lives include romantic connections, friendships, partnerships, and relationships with coworkers and teachers.

This book gives a detailed account of anxiety, types of attachments, and their effects on relationships. In addition, it will offer you insight into your love life and, most importantly, how to overcome the mental barrier which is restricting you from living your life to its fullest potential.

CHAPTER 1: EIGHT SIGNS OF ANXIETY IN YOUR RELATIONSHIP

Are you burdened by anxiety and sorrow about all the ways your relationship may go wrong? Are you stuck with thoughts like, will this last, or is this even real? This irrational and enduring fear is known as relationship anxiety, and it is something many people struggle with. Even if things are going wonderfully in your relationship, you are still constantly worried that the relationship will not last. Does this sound familiar? Do you think you may have relationship anxiety? Here are eight symptoms to look out for:

1. Insecurities

The most common manifestation of relationship anxiety is insecurity. Do you often feel like you do not belong or have no place in your partner's life? You find yourself constantly pondering if you matter to the people you love and how important you are to them. You ask yourself questions like, "Will they miss me when I am gone?" or "Will they be there for me?" You wonder if the connection you feel with them is genuine.

2. Doubts

Do you routinely doubt that your partner's feelings for you are real? No matter how many times they say that they love you, can you not help but wonder if they mean it? Even when they step out and make grand romantic gestures, you still want more reassurance to quiet all the lingering doubt in your mind, and you always need them to prove their loyalty to you.

3. Too reliant

Do you habitually find yourself staring at your phone, waiting for your spouse to text you back? Do you get scared when you do not see them and worry that they will forget about you? Do you get irritated when they spend time with someone other than you? Of course, it is normal to feel attracted to your spouse and to want to spend a considerable amount of time with them. Still, when you have relationship anxiety, it may make you clingy, and too reliant on your spouse.

4. People pleasing

You want to please your spouse so strongly that you opt to remain silent about things that concern you. You are hesitant to start any fights or arguments and instead go along with whatever your spouse wishes. If you have relationship anxiety, it will erroneously convince you that if you do not do everything you can to satisfy your spouse, they will leave you. People pleasing generally arises from unresolved abandonment problems or an unmet desire for love; you regularly prioritize their wants before your own, and you constantly go above and beyond to make others happy.

5. Overthinking

Do you replay prior discussions in your brain and beat yourself up over what you believe you should have said, getting hung up on every minor dispute and worrying that it will cause them to leave? If you have a propensity to overthink your partner's words and behaviors down to the tone of their voice and the expression on their face, this is a sign of relationship anxiety.

6. Considering yourself a failure

You beat yourself up over everything, whether it is simply forgetting to greet your significant other in the morning, missing their calls, or not being able to make it on a date. You always beat yourself up over all the ways you think you failed them as a partner. You get mad at yourself for every little mistake you make and worry that it will mean the end of your relationship, no matter how much you try.

7. Keeping your partner at an emotional distance

You are concerned that things will become too serious. Do you love your spouse but cannot commit to them because you are secretly terrified of your relationship growing more serious? Relationship anxiety may make you cautious about getting too close to someone. When they suggest things like seeing their parents, going on a trip together, or moving in with them, you want to run far, far away because you believe it is just a matter of time until the relationship falls apart and you get wounded. When there is a fear of commitment, there is unquestionably an issue.

8. Difficulty in forgiving your partner

You are constantly on the edge of your seat, waiting for anything to go wrong. You have convinced yourself that you are setting yourself up for heartbreak and disappointment due to your relationship anxieties. You have difficulty forgiving your spouse for their faults and letting things go, and you continually seek reasons to depart. You make a huge deal out of things and frighten people away easily. While you may believe you are protecting yourself, the fact is that your worry is preventing you from being joyful, enjoying the present, and giving your relationship with this person a fighting chance.

As well as these eight major signs, there are lots of other behaviors that can indicate relationship anxiety.

Some people are unable to communicate because they do not wish to comprehend the opinions of others, or because past experiences have harmed them emotionally. If, for example, you are unable to convey your sentiments to your partner, it's likely you were not previously encouraged to express your emotions. Therefore, you will have to relearn how to communicate entirely.

Some people feel much jealousy. A little jealousy is fine, but too much will cause things to come apart. Being extremely jealous is a big red flag. Jealousy does not imply that you are insane but perhaps dealing with cheaters in the past has eroded trust. Perhaps you are afraid of being abandoned, betrayed, or mistreated.

Some people have an undue desire for command and control. They believe that nothing unpleasant will happen to them or their relationship if they can control every event. This authoritarian approach will eventually drive away their loved ones.

Some people who suffer from relationship anxiety will send mixed messages. One moment they are warm and inviting, and the next, they are distant. They can change gears so fast that your head will spin.

No matter which of the above-mentioned toxic signs you see in your relationship or own behavior, be gentle. It might be because of your own or your partner's bitter past experiences, and we must learn that the past is in the past now and it is time to move on.

CHAPTER 2: UNDERSTANDING THE ROOTS OF ANXIETY

The origins of anxiety

Anxiety affects 40 million Americans over the age of 18, according to the American Anxiety and Depression Association. Most of us who endure anxiety are familiar with its symptoms, but what about its underlying causes?

Environmental factors that can trigger various types of anxiety include losing a loved one, stress in relationships, stress at work, stress in education, family history, and genetic susceptibility.

How does our brain sense anxiety?

Imagine you come across a rattlesnake.

The image is delivered to the amygdala, a portion of your brain. This is the primordial part of your brain that thinks literally. When left unchecked, it causes immediate and uncontrollable reactions. Alternatively, the hippocampus and cortex can process a stimulus in context by recalling past experiences. They allow us to react differently when we see a rattlesnake securely behind glass versus one coiled at our feet.

To put it another way, your amygdala is fast to press the gas (increasing your pulse rate and speeding up your breathing), whereas your hippocampus can press the brakes to help calm you down. Before conscious awareness, the primitive fear system kicks in approximately a tenth of second after our initial perception. When sensory data processed by the cortex enters our consciousness a fraction of a second later, the rational fear system kicks in. When we are in a risky situation, the primitive fear system causes us to be hypervigilant to any potential threat. This system evolved to suit the primordial demands of a brutal, vicious, life-or-death environment one hundred thousand years ago, a world in which most human beings died before reaching thirty.

A rising amount of data points to biological underpinnings of anxiety and panic. For example, when adrenal steroids (stress hormones) reach the hippocampus, they set off a chain reaction that eventually suppresses additional adrenal function. As a result, the hippocampus plays a crucial role in stress response modulation. According to current studies, prolonged periods of stress, such as those encountered in child abuse or neglect, produce hippocampal damage. Vietnam veterans, for example, and survivors of long-term child abuse have a smaller hippocampus and decreased memory. However, this damage appears to be reversible, as current research indicates that the hippocampus may regenerate nerve cells.

The amygdala is a brain region associated with fear and anxiety. As previously said, the amygdala receives sensory input first, and it is a warning sign of a hazard. Then it starts to prepare your body for a reaction. According to research, the amygdala has a strong memory. When a major stressful or traumatic event occurs, the amygdala records it indefinitely. Though this may seem to be an overwhelming barrier to recovery, fresh knowledge can offset it. For example, assume someone is bitten by a dog and develops a fear of dogs as a result. If that individual continues addressing friendly pets, they can generate new, more pleasant memories over time. These recollections are stored in the brain as further information, such as "most dogs do not bite." This newly acquired knowledge can then serve as a counterbalance to the amygdala's initial anxiety response.

While stress and trauma affect both the hippocampus and the amygdala, they appear to affect them differently. The hippocampus is less likely to have a vivid recollection of the experience, whereas the amygdala is more likely to have a strong and permanent recall. Thus, it is conceivable to have weak conscious memory of a traumatic incident while forming highly significant implicit, unconscious emotional memories. It is impossible to retrieve a conscious memory if it did not develop. In this case, your fear center may recall a trauma that you are unable to consciously recall.

Anxiety or panic does not imply that you are wrong or "becoming insane." On the contrary, it is a powerful indication from your subconscious that something terrifying and harmful occurred in the past and that you should be cautious in the future.

Persistent anxiety and panic are related to a variety of psychological characteristics.

Attentional focus and cognitive beliefs are the two major categories. What a person directs their attention to is referred to as attentional focus. A schema or belief system guides your interpretation of events through cognitive beliefs.

Focused Attention

There is far too much information flowing in from all of our senses to perceive everything at once. As such, you are always selectively disregarding some components of the reality in front of you. Take, for example, a bookcase with paperweights on it. An anxious person may regard the paperweights as possible blunt force weapons, whereas a non-anxious person may concentrate on the book titles.

Cognitive Beliefs

Anxiety is reinforced by believing that the world is a hazardous place, and holding that belief turns your attention away from evidence of safety and toward the threat.

When you combine this fear of danger with the notion that you will be unable to cope with the looming harm, you have a case of increasing anxiety. As worry increases, it creates tunnel vision, impairing one's capacity to analyze and appraise a situation logically. In addition, this heightened mood makes it much more difficult to detect exterior safety indicators or access reassuring recollections.

What factors might predispose someone to anxiety or panic?

Social learning, stress, and insecure attachment are three significant elements that predispose someone to anxiety or panic.

Having a history of heart attack or cancer in a family and then being frightened about having that ailment yourself would be an example of social learning.

Another key contributor to anxiety and panic is stress in early life. There is compelling evidence that early stressful life events can cause long-term changes in brain function, hence mediating the neurobiological predisposition to develop chronic anxiety and depression later in life.

The attachment type of a person is important in determining what resources they will have access to when confronted with stressful life situations. In insecure/disorganized attachment, caregivers appear to frighten their children through their negative behavior, often stemming from their own childhood experiences. When a caregiver's trauma or loss is triggered, they may act in ways that communicate their fear. It is hypothesized that this is how fearfulness is passed down through generations.

Clinical signs and symptoms of anxiety

What exactly is anxiety? If you ask anyone to characterize anxiety, you will immediately find that there is no shortage of examples. Although anxiety is a relatively typical human experience, the descriptions vary greatly.

Anxiety is a natural human feeling. It is something that everyone goes through. However, each person experiences this sensation in different ways. Common anxiety indicators include:

- Brain fog

- Irritation

- Heart palpitations

- Tension in the muscles

- Giddiness

- Recurring nightmares

- Panic attacks

Most, if not all, fears are rooted in an underlying reason. Among the most common are:

- Fear of being emotionally exposed

- Growing up with bad familial relationships

- Insecure attachment to parents or a lack of affection received as a child

- Lack of communication

- Low self-esteem/inability to accept oneself

- Previous romances that ended in heartbreak

- Fear of not being accepted or poorly regarded

- Fear of abandonment

- Marriage phobia

Biological causes of anxiety

The human body is assumed to be made up of ten interconnected systems. More than half of these ten complex systems are involved in the emergence of anxious and scared symptoms:

- The nervous system (including the brain)

- The circulatory system

- The pulmonary system

- The gastrointestinal tract

- The excretory system

- The endocrine system

These six systems oversee the physiological, electrical, and chemical changes that induce and influence anxiety symptoms. The explanations for these diverse systems can become fairly complex.

While the nervous system uses electrical signals to interact with the rest of the body, the endocrine system uses chemical messengers. Chemical messengers are categorized into two types:

1) Hormones circulate throughout the body via the bloodstream.

2) Neurotransmitters are chemical messengers that function within the brain.

Adrenal glands are a component of the endocrine system. When the CNS is active, the adrenal glands produce two hormones known as adrenaline and noradrenaline. These two compounds offer the additional fuel that the body needs while it "revs up" for activity. These two components have a lot in common. For example, they work to raise blood pressure and heart rate. Adrenaline and noradrenaline are also considered neurotransmitters because they are located in the brain.

In addition to these two, other hormones activate numerous processes throughout the body in reaction to stress. For example, the corticotropin-releasing hormone (CRH) is a stress-related hormone. To date, the majority of CRH research has been undertaken on animals (specifically rodents). According to this research, high levels of CRH are linked to anxiety-related behaviors. As a result, it has been suggested that CRH malfunction or dysregulation may produce greater anxiety in humans.

Furthermore, CRH aids in the activation of the hypothalamic-pituitary-adrenocortical (HPA) axis. The HPA is another neuroendocrine system component implicated in the stress response. It has been connected to anxiety disorders and mood disorders such as depression. While these are intriguing research areas, they are extremely complex and beyond the scope of this book. Nonetheless, our growing understanding of the human brain has helped us better comprehend mental illnesses, including anxiety disorders.

Neurotransmitters are the second most significant sort of chemical messenger. The brain's communication system is comprised of neurotransmitters. They make one nerve (neuron) communicate with another, instructing it on what to perform. Some symptoms of psychiatric diseases are thought to be caused by imbalances or insufficient levels of certain neurotransmitters. For example, serotonin is a neurotransmitter that is frequently related to anxiety. Serotonin is renowned for its ability to influence mood, appetite, and sleep. Unfortunately, serotonin levels are known to be lower in patients with anxiety disorders. As a result, drugs used to treat anxiety disorders are selective serotonin reuptake inhibitors (SSRIs). These drugs work by boosting the amount of accessible serotonin.

GABA, or gamma-aminobutyric acid, has also been related to anxiety. GABA works to "calm" the brain by slowing neuronal transmission. As a result, the body relaxes. Chronic anxiety sufferers may have a GABA deficit. It has been argued that people with this impairment may experience more anxiety because their bodies are already in a state of heightened arousal and attention, resulting in a physiological sensitivity to increasing amounts of stress. Benzodiazepines, a type of medicine commonly recommended for anxiety disorders, are hypothesized to stimulate GABA release, resulting in a relaxing effect.

During the fight-or-flight response, the body needs increased oxygen to feed the muscles. To pump more blood, the heart must beat quicker. The blood gives oxygen. Symptoms of anxiety include having heart palpitations or the fear of having a heart attack. However, certain regions of the body require more oxygen than others. As a result, the body is fuel-efficient. It restricts blood flow to areas that need it less (like your fingertips and toes). Blood flow is rerouted to where it is needed the most (like the large muscles in your arms and legs). We lose feeling in our extremities because of this.

While your thighs and biceps receive more blood flow than usual during fight-or-flight, your brain receives less. You can relax; this decrease in blood supply to the brain is harmless, and no persistent adverse consequences will occur. Nevertheless, it may create dizziness or a lightheaded sensation of unreality. It can also cause problems with memory and focus.

As the heart has to work harder to increase the amount of available oxygen, the respiratory system has to work more to raise the amount of oxygen available. Breathing must increase. Additional oxygen fuels the muscular cells. Rapid breathing gets the muscles extra energy. Tightness in the chest can also occur, as well as lightheadedness.

As well as raising respiration and heart rate, the CNS promotes perspiration. Sweating acts as the human body's AC system and keeps the body cool. The by-product of intense muscle functioning is the generation of heat. Perspiration helps this excess heat evaporate. It also makes people slick. Adding a layer of sweat could make it more difficult for your opponent to hang on to you.

There are exceptions to the rule that the CNS turns things "on" during the fight-or-flight response. Digestive processes are one such exception. To conserve fuel, it shuts down unneeded biological activities while it is in a high-alert state. Surprisingly, digestion is not necessary for this heightened state of alertness. We rarely see soldiers enjoying snacks while they are on duty. Thus, the digestive system switches "off" during fight-or-flight. Instead, the digestive system is activated by the parasympathetic nervous system (the rest-and-relaxation system). To remember this, think of how you feel after a Thanksgiving feast. What do people do? Relax, or take a nap. This focuses your body's attention on digesting that large meal.

When the digestive system shuts down, you may develop nausea or stomach aches. Furthermore, you may suffer from a dry mouth because saliva is also used for digestion. Constipation is another common effect.

Stimulation of the CNS activates the complete body. This may result in aftereffects such as tiredness. It is like running a marathon, even though your body appears to be moving around very little. On the inside, CNS activation depletes a considerable proportion of the body's fuel, causing significant weariness.

External causes of anxiety

When we talk about your surroundings, we are referring to both your natural and social environment. Environmental stressors are just one external cause of tension and anxiety.

Anxiety and anxiety disorders have various origins, but they all fall into one of two categories: hereditary or environmental. When it comes to environmental causes, biological ones are among the most manageable. Some of the most common causes of anxiety are psychotropic medications or chemicals that impact an individual's mental and emotional processes. Caffeine is the most prevalent of these drugs.

Caffeine is a nervous system stimulant that can produce racing thoughts, difficulty concentrating, rapid heartbeat, and shallow breathing, among other things. It is strongly linked to anxiety and can either induce anxious or tense sensations and actions or exacerbate pre-existing anxiety disorders. Other medications, such as methamphetamines, can produce similar feelings.

Events that occur in day-to-day life are probably the most common environmental source of worry. Anxiety is common in situations involving loss or rapid and unexpected change. For example, learning that parents are divorcing can cause significant worry in youngsters. Getting fired from a job is another example of a situation that can cause a great deal of fear and anxiety. In both examples, the future is suddenly unpredictable, and what was previously assumed to be routine and planned out is now a massive unknown.

Traumas also inflict a great deal of harm. Trauma is known to cause a wide range of symptoms, the most common of which are anxiety-related. Trauma is like a mental wound that pushes the victim to keep going as if expecting the attack or damage to happen again and again. It is exhausting to keep running at that pace.

Anxiety can arise from a variety of sources. The crucial point is that worry, no matter what causes it, is treatable. Medication, education, and therapy can all assist in minimizing the intensity of anxiety or eliminate it completely. A range of mental health providers is available to help you. Many people have had success working with a counselor via an online therapy service. These services are far easier than face-to-face appointments and can be far less costly.

CHAPTER 3: HOW DO ATTACHMENT STYLES AFFECT YOUR LIFE?

Attachment, also known as the attachment bond, is the emotional tie you made as an infant with your primary caregiver, most likely your mother. According to attachment theory, which was developed by British psychiatrist John Bowlby and American psychologist Mary Ainsworth, the level of bonding you had during your first relationship frequently impacts how well you relate to others and respond to intimacy throughout your life.

As a newborn, if your primary caregiver made you feel safe and were able to respond to your cries and appropriately interpret your changing physical and emotional requirements, you most likely built a successful, secure connection. As an adult, this usually translates to being self-assured, trusting, hopeful, able to manage conflict, respond to intimacy, and negotiate the ups and downs of romantic relationships.

If your caregiver could not consistently comfort you or respond to your demands during your infancy, you are more likely to have had a failed or insecure attachment. Infants with insecure attachment frequently grow into adults who struggle to understand their own emotions and the emotions of others, restricting their ability to form or sustain solid relationships. They may struggle to connect with others, avoid intimacy, or be overly clingy, afraid, or worried in a relationship.

Of course, our relationships are also influenced and shaped by our experiences between infancy and adulthood. However, because the attachment link has such a powerful influence on the infant's brain, understanding your attachment style can provide key insights into why you may be having trouble in your adult relationships. For example, perhaps you behave in perplexing or self-destructive ways in close relationships? Maybe you make the same mistakes over and over? Or maybe you find it difficult to make meaningful connections in the first place?

Whatever your relationship issues are, it is vital to remember that your brain can change throughout your life. You can learn to overcome your anxieties, establish a more secure way of interacting with others, and build stronger, healthier, and more satisfying relationships by discovering your attachment type.

Attachment styles or types are defined by the behavior displayed in a relationship, particularly when the relationship is threatened. For example, when faced with relationship troubles, someone with a secure attachment type may be able to discuss their feelings and seek support openly. Those with troubled attachment styles, on the other hand, may become needy or clingy in their closest relationships, act selfishly or manipulatively when they are vulnerable, or avoid connection entirely.

Understanding how your attachment style molds and influences your intimate relationships can help you make sense of your behavior, how your partner perceives you, and how you respond to intimacy. Identifying these patterns can then assist you in clarifying what you require in a relationship and the best strategy to resolve issues.

While the newborn-primary caregiver connection shapes attachment types significantly, especially during the first year, it is crucial to emphasize that attachment strength is not exclusively determined by the quantity of parental love or the quality of care that newborn receives. Attachment is also based on the nonverbal emotional communication between caregiver and infant.

An infant expresses its emotions through nonverbal cues such as crying, cooing, and, later, pointing and smiling. The caregiver, in turn, analyzes and interprets these signs, responding to the child's demand for food, comfort, or affection. A secure attachment emerges when this nonverbal communication is successful.

Attachment success is unaffected by socioeconomic criteria such as wealth, education, ethnicity, or culture. It's important to note that your parents are not solely responsible for your relationship failures. Your personality and your intervening experiences during childhood, adolescence, and adulthood can also influence your attachment type.

Attachment types

Aside from defining attachment as secure or insecure, there are subcategories of insecure attachment that result in four major attachment styles:

- Secure attachment

- Ambivalent (or anxious-preoccupied) attachment

- Avoidant-dismissive attachment

- Disorganized attachment

Secure attachment

People with secure attachment are more empathetic and capable of setting appropriate boundaries, and they feel safer, more stable, and more fulfilled in their relationships. While they are not afraid to be alone, they usually flourish in intimate, meaningful partnerships.

How does a secure attachment style influence adult relationships?

Having a stable attachment style does not imply that you are perfect or do not have relationship troubles. However, you are probably secure enough to accept responsibility for your faults and inadequacies, and you are willing to seek help and assistance when necessary.

You value your self-worth and can be yourself in an intimate relationship. You are at ease expressing your emotions, hopes, and needs.

You feel fulfillment in being with people, and you openly seek support and comfort from your partner, but you are not particularly concerned when the two of you are apart.

You are equally content for your partner to rely on you for assistance.

You can keep your emotional equilibrium and look for healthy ways to deal with conflict in a close relationship.

You are flexible enough to bounce back when faced with disappointment, setbacks, and tragedy in your relationships, as well as other aspects of your life.

Relationship with primary caregivers

As someone with a secure attachment style, your primary caregiver was likely to stay involved with you as an infant while efficiently calming and soothing you when you were distressed. As a result, they consistently made you feel safe and comfortable, connected with you through emotion, and responded to your shifting needs, allowing your nervous system to become "securely linked."

Of course, no parent or caregiver is flawless, and no one can be entirely present and attentive to a newborn 24 hours a day, seven days a week. In truth, this is not necessary in order to establish safe attachment in a child. Because of the solid basis of a healthy attachment bond, you were able to be self-confident, trustworthy, hopeful, and comfortable in the face of conflict as a youngster.

Ambivalent (or anxious-preoccupied) attachment

People with an ambivalent attachment style (also known as "anxious-preoccupied," "ambivalent-anxious," or simply "anxious attachment") are highly dependent. As the labels imply, people with this attachment style are frequently apprehensive and uncertain, with low self-esteem. They seek emotional contact yet are concerned that others may reject them.

**The impact of ambivalent attachment type on adult rela-
tionships**

You may be uncomfortable about being too attached or your
constant desire for love and attention if you have an uncertain
or anxious-preoccupied attachment style. Alternatively, you
may be worn down by dread and concern about whether your
spouse genuinely loves you.

You desire to be in a relationship and seek closeness and intimacy with your significant other, yet you do not trust or rely on
your spouse.

Being in a romantic relationship can take over your life and
cause you to become overly focused on the other person.

You may struggle to set boundaries, seeing space between you
as a threat that might cause panic, anger, or worry that your
partner no longer wants you.

Your sense of self-worth is heavily influenced by how you believe
you are being treated in the relationship, and you overreact to
any perceived dangers to the connection.

When you are separated from your partner, you may experience
anxiety or jealousy and may resort to guilt, controlling behavior,
or other manipulative measures to keep them close.

Your companion must provide you with constant reassurance and undivided attention.

Others may judge you for being too needy or clingy, and you may find it difficult to establish close connections.

Relationship with primary caregivers

Your parent or primary caregiver was most likely uneven in their parenting style, sometimes involved and sensitive to your needs and other times inaccessible or distracted. This inconsistency may have left you uneasy and unsure whether your needs in this "first" relationship would be met, serving as a model for your conduct in subsequent relationships.

Avoidant-dismissive insecure attachment style

Grown-ups with an avoidant-dismissive insecure attachment style are the opposite to those who are ambivalent or anxiously obsessed. Instead of desiring intimacy, they are so afraid of the contact that they shun emotional connection with others.

The impact of avoidant attachment style on adult relationships

You may find it challenging to accept emotional connection if you have an avoidant-dismissive attachment style. You love your self-sufficiency and freedom so much that intimacy and closeness in a romantic relationship might make you feel uncomfortable, if not suffocated.

You are a self-sufficient individual who does not feel the need to rely on others.

The more someone attempts to approach you or the more dependent a relationship becomes, the more you recede.

You are uncomfortable with your emotions, and your partners frequently accuse you of being distant and walled off, inflexible and intolerant. In response, you accuse them of being overly dependent.

To recover your sense of freedom, you may belittle or dismiss your partner's sentiments, keep secrets from them, indulge in affairs, or even abandon relationships.

You may prefer short-term, casual relationships to long-term intimate ones, or you may seek equally independent partners, who keep their emotional distance.

While you may believe that you do not require close connections or intimacy, the truth is that we all do. Humans are hardwired for connection, and even those with an avoidant-dismissive attachment style desire an intimate, meaningful relationship if they can overcome their deep-seated anxieties surrounding intimacy.

Relationship with primary caregivers

An avoidant-dismissive attachment style is frequently the result of a parent who was inaccessible or rejecting during your childhood. Because your needs were not satisfied on a consistent or predictable basis, you were forced to detach yourself and try to self-soothe emotionally. This laid the groundwork for avoiding closeness and desiring independence later in life —even when that independence and lack of intimacy creates misery.

Disorganized/disoriented attachment style

Disorganized/disoriented attachment, also known as fearful-avoidant attachment, is caused by strong fear, which is frequently the outcome of childhood trauma, neglect, or abuse. As a result, adults with this insecure attachment style believe they do not deserve love or connection in a relationship.

What effect does a disorganized attachment style have on adult relationships?

If you have an disorganized attachment style, you probably have not learned to self-soothe your emotions, so both relationships and the environment around you can feel terrifying and unsafe. If you were abused as a child, you might try to recreate abusive behavior patterns as an adult.

You most likely find intimate relationships perplexing and disturbing, frequently oscillating between emotional extremes of love and hatred for a partner.

You may be insensitive to your partner's feelings, egotistical, controlling, and untrustworthy, leading to explosive or even abusive behavior. You can be as harsh on yourself as you are on others.

You may engage in antisocial or bad behavior patterns, abuse alcohol or drugs, or be aggressive or violent.

Others may be disappointed by your refusal to accept responsibility for your actions.

While you long for the stability and protection of a meaningful, personal relationship, you also feel unworthy of love and are fearful of being harmed again.

Abuse, neglect, or trauma may have influenced your childhood.

Relationship with primary caregivers

If your primary caregiver had unresolved trauma, it might have contributed to the strong fear associated with a disorganized/disoriented attachment style. As an infant, your parent frequently served as both a source of terror and comfort for you, contributing to the confusion and disorientation you feel about relationships now. Your parental figure may also have ignored or neglected your requirements as a baby, or their erratic, chaotic conduct may have scared or traumatized you.

Insecure attachment causes

There are numerous reasons why even a caring parent may fail to establish a solid attachment bond with a newborn. Your insecure attachment could be caused by one or more of the following factors:

- Having a mother who is young or inexperienced and lacks the necessary parenting abilities.

- Your caregiver became depressed due to isolation, a lack of social support, or hormonal issues, prompting them to withdraw from the caring position.

- Because of their obsession with alcohol or other substances, your primary caregiver could not appropriately interpret or respond to your physical or emotional requirements.

- Traumatic events, such as a catastrophic sickness or an accident, might disrupt the bonding process.

- Physical neglect includes poor nutrition, insufficient exercise, and failure to address medical conditions.

- Neglect or misuse of one's emotions. For example,

your caregiver may have given little attention to you as a youngster, made little effort to understand your feelings, or verbally abused you.

- Abuse, whether physical or sexual, can result in injury or violation.

- Illness, death, divorce, or adoption may cause you to be separated from your primary caretaker.

- The primary caregiver's inconsistency. For example, you may have had a string of nannies or daycare employees.

- Moves or placements that occur frequently. For example, if you spent your childhood in orphanages or moved between foster families, you were continuously exposed to new environments.

Attachment Test and Treatment

Obtaining assistance for an insecure attachment

If you detect an insecure attachment style in yourself or your partner, it is vital to know that you do not have to accept the same attitudes, expectations, or behavior patterns for the rest of your lives. As an adult, you can modify and create a more stable attachment pattern.

Therapy can be quite beneficial, whether you work one on one with a therapist or attend couples counseling with your partner. A therapist trained in attachment theory can assist you in making sense of your prior emotional experiences and be more secure, whether alone or in a pair.

If you do not have enough resources to get suitable therapy, there are numerous things you may do on your own to develop a more secure attachment style. To begin, understand everything you can about your insecure attachment style. The more you learn, the more you will be able to identify and change the reflexive attitudes and actions of insecure attachment that may be contributing to your relationship troubles.

The following suggestions can assist you in transitioning to a more stable attachment style:

1. Enhance your nonverbal communication abilities.

One of the most fundamental insights learned from attachment theory is that adult relationships, like the first relationship you have with your primary caregiver, rely on nonverbal forms of communication to succeed.

When you engage with others, you are constantly sending and receiving nonverbal signals through gestures, posture, how much eye contact you make, and so on. These nonverbal clues convey powerful messages about how you truly feel.

Developing your ability to read, understand, and communicate nonverbally can help you strengthen and deepen your connections with others at any age. Being present in the moment, learning to manage stress, and increasing emotional awareness are ways to enhance these talents.

2. Enhance your emotional intelligence.

Emotional intelligence is the capacity to understand, use, and control your own emotions in constructive ways to sympathize with your partner, communicate more effectively, and deal with conflict in a healthier manner.

Building emotional intelligence can deepen a love connection and improve your nonverbal communication skills. Understanding and controlling your emotions can allow you to express your wants and feelings, and comprehend how your partner truly feels.

3. Establish relationships with people who have a strong attachment to you.

Being in a relationship with someone who has an insecure attachment style can result in a relationship that is out of sync at best, unstable, confused, or even painful at worst. If you are single, looking for a partner with a safe attachment style might help move you away from harmful thinking and behavior.

A solid, supportive relationship with someone who makes you feel loved might help you develop a sense of security. According to research, 50 to 60 percent of people have a secure attachment type, so you have a decent chance of meeting a love partner who can help you overcome your concerns. Similarly, building deep friendships with these people can assist you in recognizing and adopting new patterns of behavior.

4. Work through any childhood traumas.

As previously noted, trauma as an infant or young child can disrupt the connection and bonding process. Childhood trauma can be caused by anything that makes you feel uncomfortable, such as a dangerous or insecure home environment, separation from your primary caregiver, significant sickness, neglect, or abuse. Feelings of uncertainty, anxiety, and powerlessness can persist throughout adulthood if childhood trauma is not addressed.

Even if your trauma occurred many years ago, there are measures you can take to overcome the suffering, recover emotional equilibrium, and relearn how to trust and connect in relationships.

CHAPTER 4: EMPTY THE NEGATIVE THOUGHTS!

We have at least 6,000 times thoughts a day, and a few of them are likely to be negative.

The problem is, when they invade our minds, bad thoughts can block us from enjoying healthy, happy lives. Anxiety and despair commonly occur together.

In this chapter, we will focus on dealing with negative thoughts. First, the reader must learn to recognize these unpleasant thoughts, and then use the four easy techniques outlined below in order to release them:

First, step back

You are not your thoughts; you are simply clinging onto them for the time being.

They are being observed and you are providing a safe environment for them to exist in. You do not need to do anything at this point, except notice they are there.

To assist with this, we can even give our negative thoughts a name. For example, "Kali" is the destruction goddess-inspired handle I give to my negative thoughts. Oh, there's Kali. How can I help you today?

You can acquire perspective on your negative ideas in your life by creating a small divide between the core of "you" and them.

Your thoughts are simply passengers, not drivers. Furthermore, no matter how difficult they appear to be, they are only transitory.

2. Express gratitude to them

Consider your negative thoughts to be a wild, jumping, barking dog. You can try to ignore them, tell them "No," or turn on Netflix to tune them out, but they will continue to bother you until you pay attention to them.

After all, it is their job to persuade you to tune in. So, once you have identified the negative ideas, could you pay attention to what they have to say? Find a peaceful area to halt and ground yourself, whether you're at home or work.

Put your hands over your eyes and close them. Let go of your jaw. Pull your shoulders up towards your ears, then release the tension. Make room in your heart. Take a few deep breaths, going deep into your abdomen and ask yourself, "Negative thoughts, why are you here?"

The answer might surprise you. You may believe it is because of something that happened earlier in the day, but your current circumstance may remind you of a wound from your past that needs to be healed; one that is making you feel even worse.

It is fine if it is difficult for you to sit still and listen to your ideas. You may find it simpler to process these feelings or thoughts by going for a stroll in nature by yourself, journaling in a stream of mindfulness, or working with paints or colored pencils to express your negative thoughts artistically.

3. Put some effort into them

You may have heard the expression, "You have to feel it to heal it."

Negative thoughts are an opportunity to explore a suppressed emotion, such as grief, fear, or rage. Tune in to your body and try to locate where you are physically harboring these feelings.

Grief may manifest as a constriction in your chest, anxiety as a pit in your stomach, or anger as trembling in your arms and legs. Imagine sending ten deep breaths to a specific spot of discomfort in your body once you have tuned in.

This will, in a sense, put out the fire. Your autonomic nervous system will receive a powerful, soothing signal as a result. This soothes the fight, flight, or freeze response, which generates stress chemicals such as cortisol and adrenaline.

Deep breathing promotes the parasympathetic nervous system, which is your "rest and digest" mode, allowing you to think more clearly about what is upsetting you and come up with answers.

4. Thank them and make room for them

Negative thoughts exist to safeguard us. They notify us when something is not quite right with our situation. We would not know when something was "odd" if they were not there.

Negative thoughts, in a strange way, are a blessing.

Rather than driving negative thoughts away, we must understand that they are an annoying yet necessary part of being human. They are welcome to share our mental space if they do not try to run the show – that is our responsibility.

To recuperate from a system overload, treat negative ideas as a gift in unusual packaging and make time in your daily plan to sit with them in meditation.

You might not notice any difference right away, but meditation works in layers – each session builds on the previous one. You may discover that you have a lot more control over your negative thoughts over time.

How can I put these suggestions into action?

Now that you have acknowledged your negative ideas, they should have less power over you. Maybe you are ready to let them go. If this is the case, action combined with intention can be quite effective.

Make a spew letter.

Put all your bad thoughts on paper to get them out of your system.

If you are having negative thoughts about a relationship, write a letter to the person. Do not hold back, and make sure you convey whatever you need to say. Take a quiet minute to dwell with the letter after it feels finished. If you are writing a letter to someone else, envision that person sitting in front of you and read the letter aloud with all your feelings. When you are done, store it, burn it (safely), or erase it. You will not send this letter to anyone; it is just for you.

This is comparable to the traditional Hawaiian practice of forgiveness, which may also bring you serenity.

Discuss it with someone

This effortless act of getting things off your chest can sometimes make it seem like a tremendous weight has been lifted.

It can be nice to know that you are not alone in dealing with your thoughts, as someone else is sharing your burden.

Could you give it to Mother Nature?

If you live near a body of water, try writing your negative ideas on the sand. Take a few steps back and let the waves wash over the words. Imagine the unpleasant thoughts departing your head as they do so. Repeat as many times as necessary.

Make a concern box

This is a physical location where you can store your negative thoughts.

Pick up a little wooden box at an art and crafts store, or look around your house for an extra box.

Decorate it by painting or gluing magazine art to it. Make a hole in the center of the top.

Write down any negative ideas you have and put them in your worry box.

If it feels wonderful, believe you are "giving over" your bad ideas to something greater than yourself, such as a higher power, your ancestors, or the cosmos in general. Negative thoughts are no longer yours after they have been placed in that box.

Remove it by shaking it off

When animals are stressed in the wild, you will notice something interesting: they do not sit and obsess about what just happened. They simply shake out their bodies and go about their business.

Thinking negatively about something repeatedly appears to be a uniquely human tendency. Taking after animals in the wild and using your body as a technique to process tough thoughts may provide you some solace.

Consider exercising, yoga, dancing about your house, shaking out each of your limbs, or any other sort of movement that you enjoy can help calm your mind's chatter.

Physical activity has been demonstrated in studies to help with stress alleviation, among other things.

The exercise of "then what?"

Often, our negative thoughts are about whether we believe we will handle external circumstances, such as feeling out of control or wondering if we will get through this.

This activity is designed to help you mentally play through the worst-case situation. Anticipating hardship is a method with roots in Stoic philosophy.

Make a list of all the bad thoughts you are having. My spouse, for example, is unable to find another job. "Then what?" you could ask.

We are unable to pay our rent.

What happens next?

We will have to get a loan.

What happens next?

They have the option to decline.

What happens next?

We will have to rely on family members.

What happens next?

It could put a strain on our connection.

What happens next?

We will have to have a difficult chat.

What happens next?

I will feel humiliated and pressured.

Continue until you can tell the difference between what you can control and what you cannot. In addition, you may discover that the worst-case scenario is more controllable than you first believed. Of course, this is not true in all circumstances, but it may help alleviate your anxiety.

CHAPTER 5: FEAR OF ABANDONMENT: OVERVIEW, SYMPTOMS, AND TREATMENT

The overpowering fear that individuals close to you may abandon you is known as abandonment fear.

A fear of abandonment can arise in anyone. It could be founded on a terrible experience you had as a youngster or a troubling relationship you had as an adult.

Maintaining healthy relationships might be hard if you are afraid of abandonment. This paralyzing fear may cause you to isolate yourself to prevent being wounded. Or you could be unintentionally sabotaging your relationships.

The first step toward overcoming your fear to recognize why you are afraid. You may be able to overcome your worries on your own or with the help of counseling. However, fear of abandonment may be a symptom of a personality problem that requires treatment.

Abandonment phobias come in a variety of colors.

You may be concerned that someone you care about will leave and never return. You may be worried that someone may disregard your emotional needs. Either can hamper your relationships with your parents, partners, or friends.

Fear of being emotionally abandoned

Although this is less evident than physical abandonment, it is no less distressing.

We all have emotional requirements. You may feel undervalued, unwanted, and alienated if those needs are not addressed. Even when you are in a relationship with someone who is physically present, you can feel incredibly alone.

If you have been the victim of emotional desertion in the past, particularly as a child, you may live in constant terror that it will happen again.

Children's fear of abandonment

It is quite common for babies and toddlers to have separation anxiety.

When a parent or primary caregiver needs to go, they may cry, shout, or refuse to let go. Children at this age have a tough time predicting when or if that individual will return.

They grow out of their fear when they realize that loved ones do return. Most children reach this milestone by the age of three.

Anxiety over abandonment in relationships

You might be hesitant to be vulnerable in a relationship. You may have trust issues and be overly concerned about your connection. This may cause you to be skeptical about your relationship.

Over time, your worries may cause the other person to withdraw, prolonging the cycle.

Symptoms of abandonment anxiety

If you are afraid of abandonment, you may recognize some of the following symptoms and signs:

- You are overly sensitive to criticism.

- You find it difficult to trust strangers, and difficult to make friends unless you are certain they like you.

- You make a drastic effort to escape the pattern of rejection or separation in dysfunctional relationships.

- You form attachments to people too fast and then have difficulty committing to a partnership

- You work so hard to satisfy the other person.

- You blame yourself when things do not go as planned.

- You remain in a relationship even though it is unhealthy.

Causes of abandonment anxiety

If you are afraid of desertion in your current relationship, it could be because you have previously been physically or emotionally abandoned. For instance, as a child, you may have witnessed the death or abandonment of a parent or caregiver.

- Your parents may have neglected you.

- Your peers may have rejected you.

- You may have had to deal with a loved one's long-term illness.

- A loving partner may have abruptly left you or acted in an untrustworthy manner.

Such occurrences can give rise to apprehension about abandonment.

An avoidant personality disorder is a personality condition characterized by a fear of abandonment, which causes the individual to feel socially restricted or inadequate. Other signs and symptoms include:

- nervousness

- low self-esteem,

- a great anxiety of being harshly judged or rejected

- social discomfort.

- avoiding group activities, and imposing social isolation on oneself

Another personality disorder in which extreme fear of abandonment can play a role is borderline personality disorder. Other signs and symptoms to look for include:

- unstable connections

- extreme impulsiveness

- warped self-image

- mood swings and irrational rage

- difficulty being alone.

Many patients with borderline personality disorder claim to have been sexually or physically abused as youngsters. Others grew up amid tremendous conflict or had family members who suffered from the same illness.

Separation Anxiety

If a child's separation anxiety persists and interferes with daily activities, he or she may have a separation anxiety disorder.

Other indications and symptoms of a separation anxiety disorder include:

- anxiety attacks

- angst at the prospect of being away from loved ones

- refusal to leave the house without a loved one or to be left alone at home

- recurring nightmares about being separated from loved ones

- When away from loved ones, physical difficulties such as stomachache or headache can arise.

Separation anxiety disorder can affect both teenagers and adults.

Long-term consequences of abandonment anxiety

Long-term consequences of abandonment anxiety can include:

- Relationships with peers and romantic partners can be difficult.

- challenges with self-esteem and trust

- trouble with rage

- fluctuations in mood

- codependency

- intimacy phobia

- anxiety

- panic attacks

- depression

Examples of abandonment anxiety

Here are a few instances of how abandonment dread might manifest itself:

- Your fear is so strong that you will not allow yourself to get near enough to anyone in case this happens. "No attachment, no abandonment," you may think.

- You obsess over your perceived flaws and what others may think of you.

- You are the consummate people-pleaser. You do not want to risk losing someone who doesn't like you enough to stick around.

- When someone criticizes you or expresses displeasure with you in any way, you are devastated.

- When you feel cheated, you tend to overreact.

- You are insecure and unpleasant.

- You break up with a love partner before they can break up with you.

- Even when the other person requests space, you remain clingy.

- You are frequently skeptical or critical of your relationship.

Identifying and treating abandonment anxiety

Fear of abandonment is not a diagnosable mental illness, but it can be recognized and treated. Furthermore, abandonment anxiety might be a symptom of a diagnosable personality disorder or another disease that should be treated.

Resolving issues of abandonment

There are some things you may do to begin healing once you acknowledge your fear of abandonment.

Cut yourself some slack and quit judging yourself harshly. Remind yourself of all the great characteristics you have that make you an excellent friend and companion.

Discuss your fear of desertion with the other person and how it arose. However, be cautious of what you expect from others. Explain your reasoning, but do not make your fear of desertion something they have to remedy. Expect no more than what is reasonable.

Maintain your friendships and expand your support network. Strong friendships can increase your self-esteem and sense of belonging.

If you find this unmanageable, talk to a qualified therapist. Individual counseling may be beneficial to you.

How to Assist Someone Who Has Been Abandoned

Here are a few techniques to try if someone you know is afraid of abandonment:

- Begin the dialogue. Encourage them to discuss it, but do not put any pressure on them.

- Understand that their fear is real, whether it makes sense to you or not.

- Assure them that you will not desert them.

- Inquire about what you can do to assist.

- Suggest counseling, but do not push it. If they express a wish to proceed, offer to help them find a skilled therapist.

When to see a doctor

If you have tried but have not been able to overcome your fear of abandonment on your own, or if you have signs of a panic condition, anxiety disorder, or depression, consult a healthcare provider.

It is best to start with your primary care physician for a thorough examination. They can then recommend you to a mental health specialist for diagnosis and treatment.

Personality disorders, if left untreated, can lead to despair, substance abuse, and social isolation.

Takeaway Message

Your relationships may suffer because of your fear of abandonment. However, there are steps you can take to reduce your

anxiety. When abandonment anxiety is part of a larger personality disorder, it can be successfully addressed with drugs and
psychotherapy.

CHAPTER 6: BREAK FREE FROM JEALOUSY

When we care about someone, we often feel as if they are ours. At best, we use the term "mine" as a term of endearment. At worst, we carry it to an unhealthy and potentially abusive level of possessiveness. For most of us, the sense that someone belongs to us stems from our affection for them, the intimacy we share, and the essential role we play in each other's lives.

It is natural to be envious of our partner's ex. We may feel envious in partnerships because we believe the ex-partner is somehow better than us, that our spouse does not love us as much as they did another, or that they are secretly harboring a flame for someone else.

But this type of envious thinking can lead to painful thought spirals and uncomfortable feelings, undermining our confidence and the stability of our partnership. Jealousy is poisonous. It undermines the jealous person's confidence and trust in their spouse, driving them away by making them feel examined, defensive, and guarded.

Jealousy is associated with feelings of inadequacy, low self-esteem, insecurity, and anxiety. It might be profoundly ingrained and difficult to break free from. The practice of mindfulness, which involves bringing presence and nonjudgmental awareness to our thoughts, emotions, and experiences, can help us identify and then move past the cause of our jealousy.

Here are some of the reasons why jealously isn't always your fault:

1. It is "natural" to feel envious when you believe your relationship is in jeopardy. According to studies, it is uncommon not to feel envious when a partner engages in behavior that you think degrades you and breaks agreements you have made. Extreme jealousy and jealous conduct are frequently outside the "normal" range, but the point is, we have all felt jealous at some point in our lives. Jealousy is a natural reaction to activities that appear to jeopardize your relationship.

2. We are continuously bombarded with pictures in the media that lead us to believe that everyone cheats. Because this message is so ubiquitous in our culture, it may be lurking in the back of your mind unconsciously. Just look at the most famous television shows and real-life dramas involving celebrities and politicians. Cheating is one of the most popular plot lines that

captures and holds our attention. Skepticism and mistrust can be sown in our brains without our knowledge until envy manifests itself in our own lives.

3. A partner's behavior can contribute to jealousy. Your spouse may be reluctant to reveal much about himself or herself. Perhaps your partner is guarded, secretive, defensive, furious, or accusatory. If your partner acts in any of these ways, you may feel quite uneasy in the relationship and be tempted to feel envious about seemingly insignificant things.

If you want to take some steps toward curing jealousy, keep reading, and start putting the ideas we will give you into practice.

Believe in your ability to overcome jealousy

When you are dealing with jealousy in your relationship, the most important thing to remember is that you CAN STOP IT.

The first step is to accept responsibility for having a jealousy problem and make a firm commitment to resolve it, no matter what.

Many individuals "say" they want to fix this issue. Still, the sad reality is that practically everyone who suffers from jealousy will do everything but accept responsibility and commit to curing it.

Jealousy will never go unless you accept responsibility for it and make a commitment to fixing it. It will just keep hurting like salt in an open wound unless you decide to do something about it once and for all.

Taking responsibility does not imply accepting blame. Make sure you take the "blame" out of it so you can go forward with action. There are many justifications as to why people do not fix their jealousy issues even if they can do it right now, and one of the most important is that the agony hasn't gotten any worse. As weird as it may sound, for some people, the suffering hasn't become serious enough or caused enough damage to their relationships for them to throw up their hands and declare, "I've had it," and decide to end their misery.

Another issue that many people have when it comes to jealousy is that they do not believe they can repair envy. They regard it as an issue that is just a part of who they are, assuming there is nothing they can do about it. But this is simply not true. Accept responsibility for having a jealousy problem and commit to resolving it.

Other people's self-esteem creates a barrier between the misery they are currently feeling and what they want for themselves. There are a number of reasons why people may not cure their jealousy issues, including a fear of change, previous experiences with partners who cheated on them, and a lack of confidence in their current spouse. Whatever your motivation, we ask you to look beyond where you are now and envision the jealousy-free life you desire.

Determine whether your jealousy is justified

When you are jealous, you may believe your partner or spouse is doing things that are not taking place...

Or are they?

This is the first question that you must answer if you wish to stop envy.

How can you determine if your eyes are playing tricks on you?

How can you tell if your partner is or is not acting inappropriately in your relationship?

How can you tell what is true?

If you suspect your partner of cheating, it is up to you to determine whether your instincts are correct or if your mind is playing tricks on you.

Learn to live in the moment

The truth about envy is that much of it stems from what we have experienced in the past or what we fear may occur in the future rather than what is happening right now.

To overcome jealousy, you must learn to live in the present moment, not bring the past into your current life experience. When one or both persons hang on to resentments from the past—wrongs from prior relationships or their present one—and continue to punish and make the other "pay" for those hurts, it is one of the deadliest and quickest ways to kill love and a relationship. Whatever you are carrying from the past—whether you were cheated on in a previous relationship and can't get it out of your head, or your present spouse cheated on you, lied to you (or any other deep hurt), and you do not feel like you can let your guard down trust him or her as you used to, it is not easy to let go of the past.

The bad news is, if you are jealous and on guard, your entire body and mind are, and you won't let love in, even if your life (or relationship) depended on it.

The good news is, you can be strategic about opening your heart, and you do not have to do it all at once.

If your existing relationship has been marred by betrayal or other deep wounds, we wouldn't recommend handing over trust all at once. Allowing the past to dwell in the past and focusing on the current moment is vital in growing closer in your relationship.

Seek support

When you are envious, ashamed, dissatisfied with yourself, and want to crawl into a hole, the last thing you may like to do is seek help—especially from your partner.

Even though it is tough to do so, there are numerous methods to ask for assistance and subsequently take constructive actions toward learning and growth. One place to begin is to adopt the mindset that "this is what is right now; it is not how it will always be" and start looking for ways to feel better. Here are a few examples:

Examine your position objectively and begin studying for new abilities that you believe would benefit you.

This could be acquiring new communication skills. Asking for assistance may also imply acquiring a new skill to help you relax, such as joining a yoga or meditation class. It could be refocusing your attention on something you are enthusiastic about.

If you have been caught up in envy, these sentiments can be all-consuming, and you may feel as if your interests and hobbies have been pushed to the sidelines.

Identify and challenge the thoughts and stories that keep you stuck.

Every one of us has thoughts and stories that keep us hooked. We may be unaware that we have them, but they might appear to rule our every move—especially when envy is present. Many people know that their false thoughts get them into problems, but they are unsure how to stop them. One of the most common queries we receive goes something like this... "How can I stop my envious thoughts when they arise? When I am overcome with jealousy, I fall downward and can't seem to climb out." When you are in the middle of it and can't think about anything else, it can be difficult to stop your envious thoughts and stories. The key is to detect those thoughts and sensations early on before they overpower you and take control. You begin by slowing down the entire process and paying close attention to what happens inside and outside you.

Concentrate on what you want

When people get envious, they focus on what is wrong and what they DO NOT want rather than what is going right and what they DO want. We are guessing that if you are jealous, you struggle with this as well. Whether you learned it someplace in your past or not, dwelling on what is wrong tends to come easy, especially when things do not appear to be going your way. When you focus on what is wrong, you create more of what you do not want—and it grows larger.

Appreciating and focusing on what is going well and what you desire, rather than allowing incorrect, negative, jealous thoughts to control you does work, and we welcome you to try it in your own life.

Practice, practice, and practice

One of the most serious repercussions of envy is that it closes your heart. When you have jealousy issues, it closes your heart not only to your partner but to everyone else in your life as well.

When you are envious, you isolate yourself from others and build a wall around your heart that even your children can sense. When jealousy leads you to close your heart to others, it becomes impossible to fully give or receive the love you desire. If you genuinely want love in your life, you must learn to relax, begin opening your heart and find a way to feel safe—and take command of your own life. Every instant, you decide. If you have a reason to be jealous, here is a re-frame for you... Consider jealousy as an indicator that you need to pay attention to what is going on, either inside or outside of you. Whatever is going on, we ask you to relax in order to cope with what you are thinking or what is truly going on that you need to address—moment by moment.

CHAPTER 7: TEN EARLY SIGNS OF A TOXIC RELATIONSHIP

1. A lack of trust

True, it takes time to trust the other person in a new relationship fully. However, if you still cannot let go and give your emotions, flaws, and other aspects of your life to your spouse after a few months of dating, you are probably in an unhealthy relationship. A good and loving relationship makes you feel safe and secure.

2. Unpredictable behavior

Having a spouse whose behavior is unpredictable is another indirect clue that your relationship is unhealthy. They will be all over you one day, showering you with love and kisses. The next day, they will treat you as if you were an enemy for no apparent reason. They might not even pick up when you call. Unpredictable behavior is undoubtedly tiring and unsustainable.

3. Unbalance of power

Power dynamics are good indications of whether a relationship is healthy or harmful. Consider the following questions: In your partnership, who makes the majority of the decisions? Who decides where to go on dates, what to do, how to spend money, and so on? A healthy and strong relationship is one in which both sides have an equal (or nearly equal) say in all aspects of the relationship.

4. Constant scathing

A good companion brings out the best in you. They should assist you in identifying your strengths, opportunities, and flaws. A little bit of criticism is beneficial, but too much of it might be harmful.

5. Failing to accept responsibility

When you have a disagreement or a quarrel, does your partner ever own their mistake and apologize for it? Or do you find yourself carrying the burden regardless of who contributed to the fight? Take a step back and assess whether your partner truly accepts responsibility. If not, you should take the next exit before this becomes the new normal.

6. Low self-esteem

You may have had excellent self-esteem before dating this individual. People did not dare to cross your boundaries. You fell in love and immediately lost your self-confidence and self-worth. This is a strong sign that the person you are dating is not a suitable match for you.

7. Ghosting.

If your significant other disappears for days on end after a dispute, then reappears and acts as if nothing occurred, you should seriously reconsider the relationship. Ghosting is simply toxic; there is no other way to put it. This behavior is emotionally exhausting and life-sucking.

8. Lack of peace

Sometimes the easiest way to tell if you are with the right person is the sense of calm (or lack thereof) you get when dating or married to them. Your companion should make you want to go out with them, tell your friends about them, and even take them home with you. If this does not add up, you are better off without your partner.

9. Manipulation.

Manipulation is difficult to detect, especially in the early stages of a relationship. This is because it frequently manifests itself in subtle, passive-aggressive ways. If your partner attempts to influence your actions, feelings, and decisions, you are a victim of manipulation. They will persuade you to do things you do not want to do, manipulate your emotions, and impose their will on everything.

10. Isolation

Finally, toxic people try to keep their partners away from their friends, family, colleagues, and other people dear to them. It can be difficult to distinguish at first, but as it accumulates, you may discover that you have been completely alienated from the people you love and care about.

Toxicity vs. Abuse

Toxicity in a relationship can manifest itself in a variety of ways, including abuse. Abusive behavior can never be justified.

Abuse occurs in a variety of shapes and sizes. Sadly, this can make it difficult to notice, particularly if you have been in a long-term, toxic relationship.

The following indicators point to physical or emotional abuse. If you identify any of these in your relationship, you should probably end it.

This is easier said than done, but we have some resources after this section that can help.

Reduced self-esteem

Your partner holds you responsible for everything that goes wrong and makes you feel as if you cannot do anything right.

You end up feeling small, confused, ashamed, and frequently exhausted. They may even do it in public by patronizing, dismissing, or shaming you.

Anxiety and chronic stress

It is acceptable to feel frustrated with your lover or to have worries about your future together. However, it would help if you did not spend too much time thinking about the relationship or your safety and protection.

Distancing from friends and family

Dealing with a toxic relationship can force you to isolate yourself from friends and family. An abusive partner, on the other hand, may forcibly separate you from your support network.

They might, for example, disconnect the phone while you are talking or get in your face to distract you. They may even persuade you that your loved ones do not want to hear from you in the first place.

Interfere with work or study

Prohibiting you from pursuing a job or studying is a method of isolating and controlling you.

They may also try to humiliate you at work or school by raising a commotion or speaking to your boss or teachers.

Intimidation and fear

An abusive partner may erupt in wrath or employ intimidation methods, such as banging their fists against walls or refusing to let you leave the house during a quarrel.

Name-calling and insults

Verbal abuse includes insults intended to humiliate and diminish your hobbies, appearance, or accomplishments.

The following are some samples of what a verbally abusive partner might say:

"You have no value."

"No one else can ever love you the way I do."

"You are incapable of doing anything right."

Financial constraint

They may have complete control over all incoming funds, preventing you from opening a bank account, limiting your access to credit cards, or just providing you with a daily stipend.

Gaslighting

Gaslighting is a psychological method that causes you to doubt your feelings, instincts, and sanity.

For instance, they may try to persuade you that they have never been abusive, claiming that it is all in your head. Alternatively, they may accuse you of being the one with rage and control difficulties by playing the victim.

Threats of self-harm

Threatening suicide or self-harm to get you to do anything is a kind of manipulation and abuse.

Physical violence

Threats and verbal insults have the potential to develop into physical violence. When your partner pushes, slaps, or hits you, it is clear that the relationship has deteriorated.

Is it possible to save the relationship?

Many people think that toxic relationships are doomed from the start. However, this is not always the case.

What is the deciding factor? Both partners must want to change. Unfortunately, there is little chance of change occurring if just one spouse is dedicated to building healthy patterns.

Here are some more ways that you may be able to work things out:

Be ready to invest

You both must have an openness and readiness to invest in improving the connection.

This may appear as an interest in deepening conversations, or as regular blocks of time set aside for spending quality time together.

Acceptance of accountability

Recognizing prior habits that have affected the relationship is critical on both ends. It expresses a desire for self-awareness and responsibility.

Change your focus from blaming to understanding

There might be a way forward if you can both steer the dialogue away from blame and toward understanding and learning.

Acceptance of outside assistance

This is a significant one. Individual or couples counseling may be required at times to help you get back on track.

Repairing a toxic relationship will require time, patience, and devotion.

Consider that most toxic relationships emerge either because of chronic issues in the current relationship or neglected issues from previous relationships.

Here are some suggestions for getting things back on track:

Do not get caught up in the past

Yes, dealing with past occurrences will certainly be an element of healing the relationship. However, this should not be the entire emphasis of your relationship in the future. Resist the need to continuously return to unfavorable scenarios.

Consider your partner with empathy

When you find yourself craving to blame your partner for all of the difficulties in your relationship, take a step back and look at the likely motivators behind their conduct.

Have they been having a difficult time at work? Was there some family drama going on?

These are not excuses for terrible behavior, but they might help you understand where your partner is coming from.

Begin therapy

An openness to treatment can be an indication that things can be fixed. Following through on this can be crucial in making progress.

While couples counseling is a good place to start, many believe that solo treatment can also be beneficial.

Look for support and help

Look for other forms of support, regardless of whether you decide to try therapy.

Talking to a close friend or attending a local support group for couples or partners struggling with specific challenges in their relationship, such as adultery or substance abuse, could be helpful.

Engage in healthy communication

Pay special attention to how you talk to each other. Be gentle with one another. For the time being, avoid sarcasm and small barbs.

Also, emphasize the use of "I" expressions, especially when discussing interpersonal concerns.

Instead of declaring, "You do not listen to what I'm saying," you may say, "I get the impression you are not listening to me when you pull out your phone while I'm talking."

Take responsibility

Both couples must recognize their role in fostering the toxicity. This entails recognizing and accepting responsibility for your behavior in the relationship. Being present and engaged during uncomfortable conversations is also important.

Individual healing is possible

You must decide what you need from the relationship and where your boundaries are. Even if you think you already know your requirements and boundaries, it is a good idea to go over them again.

Repairing a broken relationship provides an excellent opportunity to reconsider your feelings about specific aspects of the partnership.

Allow for the other person's change

Keep in mind that things will not change suddenly. Focus on being flexible and patient with one another as you mature.

CHAPTER 8: BOOST YOUR SELF-ESTEEM

Self-esteem describes how you feel about yourself or your perception of yourself. Everyone experiences periods when they feel down or find it difficult to trust in themselves. However, if this continues for a prolonged period, it can lead to complications, including mental health issues such as sadness or anxiety. Some of the symptoms of poor self-esteem can also be indicators of these issues.

Self-esteem is frequently the product of a lifetime of experiences, especially what happened to us as youngsters. However, you can boost your self-esteem at any age. This chapter contains further information about self-esteem as well as some steps you may take to increase it.

Understanding Your Self-Esteem

Some people consider self-esteem to be their inner voice (or self-dialogue) — the voice that informs you whether you are capable of doing or achieving something.

Self-esteem refers to how we value ourselves and our perceptions of who we are and what we can do.

It is not ability that determines one's self-esteem. Self-esteem is frequently unrelated to either your abilities or other people's judgments of you. It is entirely conceivable for someone who excels at something to have low self-esteem. Someone who struggles with a specific task, on the other hand, may have high self-esteem in general.

People that have high self-esteem are often optimistic about themselves and their lives. This makes them considerably more robust and capable of dealing with life's ups and downs.

Those with low self-esteem, conversely, are frequently more critical of themselves. They have a more difficult time recovering from hardships and setbacks. As a result, they may avoid difficult circumstances. However, this might lower their self-esteem even more because they feel even worse about themselves as a result.

A lack of self-esteem can affect how people behave and what they achieve in their lives.

Why Do People Have Low Self-Esteem?

There are a few justifications for why someone may have poor self-esteem. However, it frequently begins in childhood, possibly with a sense of being unable to live up to expectations. It can also be the product of adult experiences such as a poor personal or professional relationship.

Domestic violence and abuse victims frequently have low self-esteem. This could be because their abuser has spent time mocking them and making them feel horrible about themselves. It is also possible that their poor self-esteem made them more prone to abuse because they did not believe they were valuable.

Life events that are traumatic, such as divorce or bereavement, can also negatively impact your self-esteem.

Enhancing Your Self-Esteem

There are numerous things you may do to boost your self-esteem.

1. Recognize and Question Your Negative Beliefs

The first step is to recognize and then question your unfavorable self-perceptions.

Take note of your self-perceptions. For example, you might think, "I'm not bright enough to do it," or "I do not have any friends." When you do this, look for evidence that contradicts those claims. Make a note of both the statement and the facts and return to it frequently to remind yourself that your negative thoughts about yourself are untrue.

2. Recognize the Good in Yourself

It is also a nice idea to jot down positive things about yourself, such as your ability to play a sport or compliments from others. When you are feeling down, remember these things and remind yourself that there's a lot of good in you.

In general, the positive internal conversation is an important aspect of increasing self-esteem.

If you notice yourself saying things like 'I'm not good enough' or 'I'm a failure,' you can begin to turn things around by stating things like 'I can beat this' and 'I can grow more confident by viewing myself in a more positive light.'

You will notice yourself relapsing into old negative behaviors at first, but you can begin to feel more optimistic and develop your self-esteem with consistent work.

3. Develop Positive Relationships—and Avoid Negative Relationships

You will most likely discover that certain people—and particular relationships—make you feel better than others.

If you can, avoid folks who make you feel horrible about yourself.

Build connections with people who make you feel great and avoid partnerships that make you feel bad.

4. Take Some Time Off

You do not have to be always perfect. You do not even have to like yourself all of the time.

Self-esteem changes depending on the situation, the day, and the hour. Some people are at ease and optimistic when they are around friends and colleagues, but they are uneasy and shy when they are with strangers. Others may feel completely in control at work but struggle socially (or vice versa).

Allow yourself a rest. We all have those moments when we feel low or struggle to retain our self-belief.

The idea is to not be overly critical of yourself. Be kind and try not to be too hard on yourself.

Avoid criticizing yourself in front of others since it might reinforce your negative beliefs while also giving them a (perhaps erroneous) poor opinion of you.

You can help enhance your self-esteem by rewarding yourself after completing a difficult task or simply getting through a particularly difficult day.

5. Develop Assertiveness and the Ability to Say No

People who have poor self-esteem frequently find it difficult to advocate for themselves or say no to others.

Because they do not like to say no to anyone or anything, they may feel overburdened at home or work. However, this can exacerbate stress and make it much more difficult to handle.

Developing your assertiveness might aid in the improvement of your self-esteem. In addition, acting as if you believe in yourself can sometimes help you believe in yourself more!

6. Enhance Your Physical Fitness

When we are fit and healthy, it is much easier to feel good about ourselves.

On the other hand, people with poor self-esteem frequently ignore themselves because they do not believe they "deserve" to be cared for.

Try getting more exercise, eating healthy, and sleeping enough. It is also a wonderful idea to set aside time to unwind and do something you want to do rather than something that someone else expects you to do. You may discover that small modifications like this can have a significant impact on your overall view.

7. Accept New Challenges

People who have poor self-esteem frequently avoid difficult situations. Taking on a challenge might be a good approach to boost your self-esteem. This does not imply that you must do everything yourself—part of the challenge may be to seek assistance when necessary—but be prepared to do something that you know will be tough to achieve.

By succeeding, you demonstrate to yourself that you are capable of achieving.

This will challenge your negative beliefs and, as a result, boost your self-esteem.

The Value of Small Steps

It is extremely improbable that you will shift from having low self-esteem to having high self-esteem overnight.

Instead, you will most likely make incremental improvements over time. Again, the key is to look at the broad picture rather than the details of how you felt at a particular moment and focus on the big picture.

Celebrate when you feel good or do something nice, but do not beat yourself up if you occasionally revert to negative thought patterns. Simply get back up and attempt to think more positively. This will eventually become a habit, and you will notice that your self-esteem quietly improves.

Exercises

Ask yourself a few questions!

Here are a few things you may ask yourself to increase your self-esteem and confidence right now:

- What can you do to strengthen or balance your emotions? Conversely, what can you refrain from doing?

- How would you think three months from now if you stayed on track with your goal? What change would it make in your life?

- What one simple action can you do this week to feel more in control of your life?

- What are your areas of interest? What kinds of things excite, motivate, or pique your interest? What can you do on a daily or weekly basis to nourish these passions?

- Consider occasions when you were motivated and confident. What were you up to, who were you with, and where were you going?

- What actions can you take to begin building a stronger relationship with yourself? What obstacles do you believe you must overcome to get self-acceptance and confidence?

- Do you experience conflicts with your family, friends, or coworkers? What are your choices for dealing with them?

- What kinds of activities pique your interest? Which ones make you the happiest? How can you incorporate more fun and interesting events into your next few days?

- What habits, if any, do you need to modify this year to increase your happiness and confidence? What is one habit you can start working on in the next few days? What would it be like to do this daily?

- What can you do to strengthen your bonds with friends and family?

- Who are the people in your life who will encourage you to pursue your aspirations and goals? How can you give more time to them?

- What is preventing you from feeling happy? What steps can you take to close the gap?

- What adjustments could you make in terms of money and finances to feel more financially confident?

- How can you cut your spending this month? How

would you feel about yourself because of this?

- How would you feel if you committed to one healthy behavior for the next few months? What difference would that make in your life?

Do not worry if you can't answer all of the questions. Instead, answer the questions you feel comfortable answering and return to the list later. The more you work on these, the more self-assured you will become.

Self-esteem and self-confidence affect all areas of our life, from how we hold ourselves (body language) to our chances of developing mental health disorders like depression and anxiety, and even our chances of earning a promotion or raise.

While times of low self-esteem are normal, if you are regularly experiencing emotions of worthlessness or feel as if you are a continual failure, you may be suffering from a more significant mental health issue.

Whether you have always had low self-esteem or it is a new aspect in your life, the following exercises will help educate your mind to recognize the good in everyday situations and remind you that you are valued:

1. Make yourself a priority

Your parents undoubtedly taught you as a child that it is a virtue to put other people's demands ahead of your own and that putting oneself first is selfish. While it is necessary to be giving and loving, doing so at the expense of your own needs can be quite damaging to your self-esteem.

It is critical to schedule time for yourself in your daily life. Keep in mind that you cannot help anyone if you are exhausted or ill, so taking a break allows you to be your best.

It is all right to say "no" now and then!

2. Be gentler with yourself

Let us face it: many of us do not use the nicest language when we talk to ourselves. Whether you are dissatisfied with your appearance when you look in the mirror, or you often criticize yourself for perceived "failures," the way we talk to ourselves has a significant impact on our self-esteem and mental health.

An excellent strategy for breaking the habit of negative self-talk is to intentionally declare "STOP" anytime you detect critical thoughts, then play devil's advocate with yourself.

When you detect negative thoughts coming in, jot down five things you like about yourself. For example, if you despise your butt, concentrate on the areas of your body that you like: perhaps you have great hair, piercing eyes, a pleasant smile... If you focus on these things, you might be surprised at how many positives you can think of!

3. Be willing to overlook errors

When we make mistakes, we are often considerably worse on ourselves than we would be on others. However, remember that making a mistake does not imply that you are a failure as a person. `We all make errors from time to time.

A helpful strategy for helping you forgive yourself is to modify your thinking about mistakes: instead of viewing them as failures, consider them opportunities to learn by analyzing where you went wrong and where you can improve the next time. This turns the mistake into a chance for self-improvement, which should boost your self-esteem right away.

4. Recognize success

Recognizing your triumphs is just as crucial as dealing with your mistakes. Being modest may be regarded as a virtue, but there is no shame in acknowledging a job well done (even if your supervisor or family members are not as responsive as they should be — we have all been there!).

Avoid statements like "it wasn't a big deal" or "anyone could do it" (even when talking to yourself), as these minimize your successes. It is fine to be happy with yourself.

Listing previous accomplishments can also help you recognize how much you have developed and improved over time, as well as how many successes you have had along the path, reminding you that you can and will do it again.

5. Show gratitude

Gratitude and mindfulness can be trigger words these days, and it seems like everything we read on the internet is extolling the virtues... However, there is a reason for this: it works!

Practicing thankfulness can not only help you overcome poor self-esteem but will also provide a valuable boost to all aspects of your mental health, making you feel happier and more fulfilled.

While many individuals will tout the benefits of keeping a gratitude diary, one social media challenge from 2014 provides an alternate approach to shift your mentality and focus on the good aspects of your daily life: the #100HappyDays challenge.

This challenge mixes responsibility with the necessity to focus on the positive, and every participant reported feeling happier and more fulfilled after completing it.

6. Get your body moving.

Many studies show a correlation between excellent mental health and physical activity that is impossible to ignore!

Getting your body moving and your heart pounding, whether you are out for a run, practicing yoga, or simply doing yard work, has been shown to increase mood, boost self-esteem, and help you live a happier life.

Not only is exercising necessary for a healthy mindset, but the obvious features of toning up can also enhance your self-esteem if you suffer from a negative body image. Even if you have not lost/gained weight yet, knowing that you are doing something about it can be quite beneficial.

7. Give generously

While it is important to say no to people and prioritize your needs, being generous can increase your self-esteem by demonstrating that you have something to contribute.

Helping others has been demonstrated to provide people with a feeling of meaning and purpose in life, whether it is building houses for the homeless, giving blood, or simply being helpful in general.

You might mix giving with exercise and volunteering with a charity that demands you to work out. Walking dogs for a local shelter, constructing houses, collecting contributions... There are many ways to become engaged with organizations you care about while also getting in shape!

8. Sports in groups

Team sports are fantastic for enhancing your self-esteem and mental health since they promote teamwork, cooperation, the opportunity to succeed, and are a lot of fun!

Most areas have various team sports in which you can participate in, or you can always establish your own!

9. Make a commitment

Whatever activities you pick to increase your self-esteem and mental health, you must stick with them if you want to see results. Begin with simple, attainable goals and work your way up. The achievement of meeting and exceeding your goals will increase your self-esteem in addition to the benefits of the workouts themselves!

CHAPTER 9: NATURAL REMEDIES FOR ANXIETY RELIEF AND MANAGEMENT

Even in its mildest manifestations, anxiety can be crippling. While prescription medications may be effective for some, others may seek natural anxiety and stress relief.

Anxiety symptoms include anxiousness, apprehension, and worry. Many people who do not have anxiety disorders are unaware that telling someone to "just calm down" is not a helpful therapeutic strategy (so do not say it, folks).

It is all about discovering strategies to self-soothe when dealing with worry, stress, and even panic attacks. These natural anxiety cures may be your ticket to finding some peace during your stress storm. Here are a few suggestions:

1. Get your feet moving!

Not everyone enjoys movement, but having an exercise regimen that caters to your body's demands can be beneficial.

Learning TikTok dances, water-walking with the Silver Sneakers, mastering a new yoga pose, or traversing unfamiliar terrain are all examples of movement. Exercise that you enjoy can increase endorphins, sometimes known as the "happy hormone." Sex also releases endorphins, so move your body however you want in order to reach your joy.

2. Vitamin D

Sunlight can be beneficial to your health. Serotonin levels can be diminished by a continuous absence of sun exposure, such as during a lockdown.

Serotonin is a mood-boosting hormone that can make you feel more focused and relaxed. If you cannot obtain direct sunshine and Target's kiddie pools are still out of stock, you can attempt an at-home light therapy treatment.

3. Pet the sweetest boy

If you are trawling Facebook groups for cute dog photographs, you might be missing out on the very real impact of cuddling a pet.

According to a 2015 study, sensory events such as petting a dog can cause the release of oxytocin. This can assist in alleviating stress and improve general well-being. So, tell Spot to settle in since you require some snuggle time.

4. Take it easy on the caffeine

For those who have motto "But first, coffee," your caffeine consumption may be contributing to an increase in tension and anxiety. Anyone else gets the jitters? Caffeine was found to increase anxiety, aggression, and symptoms in psychiatric patients in a 2005 study.

5. Make friends with herbal tea

To wean yourself off coffee, try introducing herbal tea into your daily regimen. These caffeine-free beverages are available in a range of flavors.

Some herbal teas are sleep aids, while others are natural anxiety and stress relievers. Both chamomile and lavender are well-known for their anxiety-relieving properties.

6. Get more rest

Despite what the rise-and-grind society would have you believe, sleep is beneficial to your health, and a lack of sleep can affect stress and anxiety levels.

The typical advice is to get 7 to 9 hours of restorative sleep per night. Insomnia is a distinctive sign of anxiety. Limiting screen time and caffeine intake at night and choosing a bedtime for yourself can help you get back on track with your sleep.

7. Try aromatherapy

Aromatherapy is a natural stress and anxiety treatment that has been used for thousands of years. Aromatherapy can be experienced in various ways, including through the sense of smell and skin application.

For natural anxiety relievers, the National Association for Holistic Aromatherapy recommends clary sage, lavender, neroli, Roman chamomile, and rose.

Remember that the FDA does not regulate essential oils. So make sure you only buy from trusted sellers.

8. Be mindful of your meditation

One of the most common reasons people practice meditation is to relieve stress. Meditation, as a mindfulness practice, has been demonstrated to lessen the inflammatory response caused by stress. According to a 2013 study, mediation had the greatest influence on individuals who were the most anxious.

Mediation is at your fingertips when you have a smartphone. Many mental health apps provide specific guided meditations for stress and anxiety. Certain meditations can even be used to control your breathing during a panic attack and return your body to a more controllable state.

9. Experiment with different breathing techniques

When you have a panic attack, you may notice that your heartrate rises and your breathing becomes more difficult to catch. Box breathing is a technique that can be used as a natural anxiety treatment. This four-step procedure aids in stress reduction and mood enhancement.

Sit up straight and exhale gradually through your mouth to get all the air out of your lungs.

Slowly inhale for four seconds through your nose, filling your lungs with air one part at a time until it feels like it is moving into your abdomen.

- For four seconds, hold your breath.

- Exhale for four seconds via your mouth, releasing the air from your lungs and abdomen.

- Hold your breath for four seconds more.

- Repeat the procedure four times.

10. Try Journaling

Chronic anxiety can erode your sense of reality, causing you to doubt yourself and others around you. To focus on facts rather than anxieties, journaling can be a useful technique for getting your thoughts back on track.

11. Rehearse 5, 4, 3, 2, 1

If you suffer frequent panic attacks, a therapist may advise you to practice a grounding technique known as "5, 4, 3, 2, 1," which helps you reconnect with reality.

Look for five objects that you can observe in your surroundings.

Observe four objects you can touch in your immediate surroundings.

Pay attention to three things you can hear around you.

Find two things that you can smell in your surroundings.

Consider something you can taste.

12. CBD is as simple as 1, 2, 3

Cannabidiol Oil, or CBD, is a marijuana plant derivative. Unlike its cannabis sister marijuana, CBD does not often include THC (what gets you high).

CBD can be bought in tincture or gummy form at natural health stores. CBD is still a relatively novel compound, but preliminary research indicates that it may be useful in treating anxiety and stress.

Beware, buyer: CBD may include trace levels of THC, which may cause you to fail a drug test.

13. Say hello to ashwagandha

The Ayurvedic herb ashwagandha may be a standout among the many natural therapies for anxiety. A 2014 study on the herb found it reduced stress and anxiety in both patient reports and secondary measures.

Natural panic attack treatments

Panic attacks cannot kill you but try explaining that to someone who is gasping for air in the midst of one. The sensation can be startling, intense, and terrifying. Chronic panic attacks can have long-term health consequences.

When you feel a panic attack coming on, here are a few natural cures:

- Can you give it a name? By labeling what is happening as a panic attack, you remind yourself that you have survived similar situations in the past and that it will not last.

- Concentrate on your breathing. Connecting with

your breath can be a powerful grounding method. Take deep belly breaths or try box breathing and continue until your body begins to settle down.

- Change your focus. Panic attacks can cause you to lose your sense of reality. Concentrate on anything stable in the room and reconnect with your surroundings.

- Make a gesture with your hands. Having a tactile reaction to worry or panic can be grounding as well. This might be as easy as holding an ice cube or as difficult as completing a whole adult coloring book.

When should you seek assistance?

Anxiety problems are prevalent, but you do not have to suffer in silence. If natural anxiety solutions do not work and symptoms linger, see a medical expert determine the best next steps.

The following are major indicators that it is time to seek help:

- Your employment or relationships are being harmed by your anxiety or panic attacks.

- You are frequently ill or in discomfort.

- You have developed anxiety or panic episodes after starting a new drug.

- You are depressed.

In conclusion

There are numerous natural anxiety treatments available. Because panic, tension, and anxiety appear differently in each person, not every strategy will work for everyone. Change your routine and discover which make you think more calmly and feel more in control.

CHAPTER 10: ANTI-ANXIETY EXERCISES

Anxiety affects practically everyone at some point in their lives. These exercises may assist you in relaxing and finding relief.

WHY ARE ANXIETY EXERCISES EFFECTIVE?

They address your body's stress responses, such as elevated heart rate, rapid breathing, and stiff muscles, and helps your body feel calm.

1. Breathe deeply to unwind.

When you are anxious, you may notice that your heartrate and respiration rate increase. You might also start sweating and feel dizzy or lightheaded. When you are anxious, controlling your breathing can help to relax both your body and mind.

Follow these strategies to regain control of your breathing when you are anxious:

- Sit somewhere peaceful and comfortable. Put your one

hand on chest and the other on your stomach. When you take a big breath, your stomach should move more than your chest.

- Inhale slowly and steadily through your nose. As you breathe in, keep an eye on and feel your hands. The hand on your chest should be stationary, but the hand on your stomach should move slightly.

- Slowly exhale through your mouth.

- Repeat this activity at least ten times or until you see a reduction in your anxiety.

2. Unwind by visualizing

Have you ever heard the phrase "finding your happy place"? Painting a mental picture of a relaxing location can genuinely help to relax your brain and body.

When you begin to feel apprehensive, find a quiet and comfortable spot to sit. Consider your perfect area to unwind. While it might be any location on the planet, actual or imagined, it should be a picture that you find particularly calming, pleasant, serene, and safe. Make it simple enough that you can refer to it when you are feeling nervous in the future.

Consider all the minor nuances you would discover if you were there. Consider how space might smell, feel, and sound. Imagine yourself in that location, relaxing and enjoying yourself.

Close your eyes and take calm, regular breaths through your nose and out of your mouth after you have a good picture of your "happy spot." Continue to focus on the place you have envisioned in your mind and be conscious of your breathing until you feel your worry subside. When you are feeling worried, go to this spot in your mind.

3. Relax your muscles

When you are nervous, you may experience muscle tightness or tension. This muscle tension can make it more difficult to manage your worry. You may lessen your anxiety levels by releasing the stress in your muscles.

To immediately release muscle tension during anxious periods, do the following:

- Sit somewhere peaceful and comfortable. Focus on your breathing while closing your eyes.

- Slowly exhale through your nose and in through your mouth.

- Make a tight fist with your hand. Squeeze your fist hard.

- Hold your fist in place for a few seconds. Take note of all the tightness in your hand.

- Slowly open your fingers and notice how they feel. You may experience a release of tension in your hand. Your hand will eventually feel lighter and more relaxed.

Continue tensing and then relaxing different muscle groups in your body, such as your hands, legs, shoulders, or feet.

4. Unwind by counting

Counting is an easy technique to relieve stress. First, find a peaceful and comfortable spot to sit when you feel anxiety rushing over you. Then, shut your eyes and count up to ten slowly. If required, repeat the process and count to 20 or a greater number. Count until you feel your anxiety subside.

This relief can come immediately at times, but it could also take a while. Maintain your cool and patience. Counting can help you relax since it gives you something to focus on other than your worry. It is an excellent technique to employ in a crowded or bustling environment, such as a store or train, when other anxiety exercises may be more difficult to carry out.

5. Unwind by remaining in the present

Mindfulness is the gentle and judgment-free practice of being present in your current state and circumstances. When your thoughts are racing, and your anxiety is growing, staying present might help you achieve a peaceful frame of mind.

To move out of your thoughts and into the present moment:

Close your eyes and find a peaceful and comfortable location to sit.

Take note of how your breathing and body are feeling.

Change your focus to the feelings you notice in your environment. Ask yourself, "What is going on outside of my body?" Take note of what you hear, smell, and feel.

Change your focus from your body to your surroundings and back again multiple times until your anxiety begins to subside.

6. Unwind by interrupting your nervous thoughts

When you are anxious, it is not always easy to think clearly. Anxious thoughts can sometimes lead us to believe damaging, incorrect things or act in ways that exacerbate our worry. It can be beneficial to break or interrupt your nervous thoughts so that you can think clearly and respond correctly to them.

Here is how to end the loop of worrying thoughts:

Consider whether you are bothered by constant concern. If the response is yes, you are now aware of it.

Experiment with several methods of disrupting your worried thought process, such as:

Singing a ridiculous song about your worry at a fast speed or speaking about your fears in a hilarious voice.

Instead of your anxiety, choose a pleasant thought to concentrate on. This could be someone you adore, your favorite place, or even something you look forward to doing later that day, such as having a delicious meal.

Read a book or listen to music.

When you move your focus from your concern to the task at hand, pay attention to how you feel.

ARE YOU FEELING WORSE?

Anxiety exercises may not be effective for everyone and may worsen symptoms in persons with generalized anxiety disorder (GAD). Consult your doctor for more effective treatment choices if you have GAD.

Anxiety can interfere with one's thoughts and activities, and it might be difficult to overcome anxiety. But know that you can find relief, even if you feel trapped. Try one of these anxiety exercises the next time you are feeling anxious.

Also, have a look at the some of the anxiety apps available today. These applications provide a variety of treatments ranging from nature sounds to acupressure instructions. However, if your anxiety frequently interferes with your everyday life, happiness, and activities, you should get additional assistance from a mental health professional.

CHAPTER 11: COUPLES EXERCISES

This chapter includes some of the finest couples therapy exercises and activities for couples who wish to strengthen their relationship with tools they can use at home.

The strong exercises will aid in the development and (re)building of trust while also improving communication and listening skills.

The exercises incorporate various treatment modalities, including cognitive behavioral therapy (CBT), positive psychology, and mindfulness-based therapies. All of these distinct approaches complement and function well together.

We have included exercises for developing trust, deepening connections, overcoming obstacles, raising awareness, and increasing communication. Some can be used in therapy sessions, while others function well as homework in couple's therapy.

Exercises and Activities for Couples Therapy

1.) The Starter

Icebreakers can be a terrific way to start an engaging conversation and learn something new about one another. It is an excellent exercise to do at the start of every couple's therapy or relationship counseling session.

Some icebreaker questions include:

What is a hilarious tale you have not told me?

Could you tell me about your childhood or an anecdote?

When you were a kid, what did you want to be?

What embarrassing experience from your life would you like to share with me?

2.) Let's be honest here.

The rules for this exercise are simple. First, both partners should be truthful in their responses to each other's questions. This will strengthen their bond with one another. Second, you can start with generic, easy-to-answer questions and work your way up to philosophical, thought-provoking ones:

What is your favorite memory from our time together?

What is your favorite service I provide for you?

What is one thing you are relieved you'll never have to do again?

When you reflect on your childhood, what memory comes to mind?

What would you do first if you awoke tomorrow without fear?

What is one type of behavior that you will never tolerate?

What would you alter about the way you were raised if you could?

What made you fall in love with me?

3.) Experiment with the Trust Fall

The trust fall is an activity in which one person stands straight, shuts their eyes, and falls without trying to stop, trusting their partner to catch them. It is, as the name implies, a trust-building activity that requires some bravery.

4.) Tell us about your favorite music.

Each couple is asked to share three songs that they enjoy. They should also try to clarify the songs' meanings. Then, listen to the tracks as a group.

What does it make you think of?

What emotions arise as a result of listening?

What mood do you generally listen to it in?

Music is incredibly personal, and this practice is a terrific opportunity to open up and connect with your partner while also expressing some vulnerability. Perhaps the couple has "their" song. Both can express the sentiments and emotions that arise when listening in this scenario.

5.) How much do you know about me?

Make a simple test to see what the couple knows about each other. After answering one question, it is the turn of the other partner. Here are some examples of questions:

What is it that gives me a sense of aliveness?

What makes me happy?

What frightens me?

What would my ideal vacation look like?

6.) Favorite book activity

Request that the couple trades their favorite books. They should discuss what they like best about this book in particular. How did it affect their lives?

Reading the partner's favorite book might provide an opportunity to gain insight into the partner's thoughts and better understand each other. Discussing the book and its impact is a terrific method to strengthen the couple's bond. This is an excellent homework assignment.

7.) Relationship Evaluation

The Relationship Assessment is an early-stage couple therapy task. Each spouse is asked to answer some basic relationship questions. It is a questionnaire that aids in the exploration of issues and problems.

It provides some basic background information about the couple. You'll learn how long the clients have known each other and learn about previous relationships or marriages. You will also learn about their family background, and any stressors contributing to the relationship problem.

8.) Recognize Relationship Issues

This is another excellent practice for the early stages of relationship coaching or couple's therapy. The exercise allows you to discover specific areas where you and the partner can improve. It consists of a series of questions that each partner must answer individually.

Each spouse may identify distinct issues in their relationship. Therefore, it is a homework assignment that must be completed before or after the first session.

Note the significant issues that each partner mentions in this questionnaire and discuss what needs to be changed.

Financial, communication, child-rearing, decision-making, jobs, controlling each other... are all potential causes of conflict in a relationship.

9.) Establish Relationship Objectives

Couple's therapy is about more than just difficulties; it is also about setting goals. It is critical to discover common ground in a partnership. Something for which both partners are willing to put in the effort. Remember that a goal should always be SMART.

A SMART goal is defined as:

Specific (Is your objective overly broad? Make it clear!)

Measurable (How can the outcome be measured?)

Attainable (Can we achieve our goal?)

Realistic (Is our goal attainable?)

Time-Bound (We wish to accomplish our goal before...)

10.) The Problem-Solving Roadmap

After identifying the relationship issues, it is time to address them one by one. The first step is to relate the individual problem to real-world scenarios. This will improve knowledge of the problem's origins and nature. Once this is completed, it is time to approach the situation and devise strategic solutions. This practice encourages the couple to come up with novel solutions. The problem-solving blueprint is best used following the exercise in which you have selected the most pressing issues that need to be addressed. Outlines the problem, describe it in a real-life scenario and is challenge yourselves to develop a creative solution.

11). The Check-In

This is an essential practice in every marriage or couple's therapy. Each pair should take a seat separately. They should pen down what has gone well since the previous session, what changes they noticed, and what they want to discuss in the upcoming session. It is a brief progress report that allows each partner to prepare for their session in only a few minutes.

12.) Gold Nuggets Therapy Session Exercise

This is an excellent addition to the pre-session check-in procedure. Take some time to write down and share your main takeaways from each session.

Possible questions include:

What did you take away from this session?

The most useful insight was...

What do you aim to achieve before the next session?

13.) The Relationship Diary

Keeping a daily relationship journal (daily/weekly) is an excellent exercise for getting to know each partner's unique perspectives.

A successful partnership requires two people. This will reveal many significant insights if both partners begin journaling about their ideas, feelings, experiences, mistakes, triumphs, and wishes.

It is also a great chance to point out and keep track of the traits and behaviors you and your partner do not like in each other.

14.) Do Not Underestimate Your Qualities and Strengths!

Too frequently, we focus on what is wrong and what does not work. This practice prompts you to examine your abilities more closely. Understanding and being aware of one another's strengths may be a big confidence booster. Sometimes we are certain of our abilities, but our partner may not notice them or take them for granted. It is also likely that something we consider our strong suit (e.g., "I'm a very organized person") is perceived completely differently by our spouse without our knowledge (e.g., "He/She is a control freak").

To begin, ask yourself, "What three major strengths do I believe my spouse would claim I have?"

What are the qualities we should work on as a couple?

15.) The PIT-Stop

De-escalate any disagreements with your partner as soon as possible.

Even the best couples have disagreements from time to time; that happens when two people who care about each other spend a lot of time together. Unfortunately, disputes can swiftly develop in some circumstances, turning a minor disagreement into a major issue.

The PIT-Stop exercise will assist you in de-escalating any pending disagreement or brawl. It is a simple approach that allows you to take a step back and become aware of your surroundings and emotions. Once the feelings have subsided, you can then handle the subject calmly.

When an argument arises, employ a keyword such as Pause, Stop, or PIT-Stop and then leave the situation. Then records your ideas and feelings on paper. Communication and the ability to listen to one another are essential for any relationship to succeed.

16.) The Mysterious Question

In coaching and counseling, the miracle question is a terrific thought experiment. The question originated in solution-focused therapy and was named by Steve de Shazer and Insoo Kim Berg. The emphasis is on the future, on the goal that the client wants to achieve.

This question assists a couple in becoming aware of their dreams and desires and learning about their partner's dreams and desires. It can be beneficial in determining what you both require to be satisfied in the relationship.

Imagine that while you were sleeping tonight, a miracle occurred: all of your current issues vanished. What would life be like?

17.) Non-Interrupted Listening

This well-known couples counseling activity emphasizes both verbal and nonverbal communication. Set a three-minute timer. One partner has the opportunity to speak freely about whatever they are thinking or feeling. The other partner is not permitted to speak but may express empathy and understanding through nonverbal means.

After three minutes, both parties can talk about their experiences, feelings, and observations. Then it is time to trade roles so that each partner may practice listening.

18.) Please Send Me a Letter

Each partner is required to compose a letter to the other. It can convey their frustration, feelings, or desires. Many people find it simpler to communicate their thoughts and sentiments in writing rather than in front of others. Each couple is then requested to respond to their partner's letter in writing.

19.) Developing into the Best Partner I Can Be

This activity will assist each couple in determining what they can do to develop their relationship skills and become the best partner they can be.

First, we must accept responsibility for our actions and refrain from blaming everything on our relationship, even if it seems like our partner is the source of the problem. Instead, we should examine ourselves and see what we can do to become the best partners we can be.

20.) Meet Your Own Needs in Your Relationship

A happy relationship is built on our comprehension of our partner's requirements. It is equally critical to recognize and communicate our own needs. The ties will fail sooner or later if both partners ignore each other's needs.

The partnership will only have a future if both partners' joint and individual needs are addressed. A sense of security, admiration and shared sensations of love, compassion, and affection are all common demands in a partnership.

Each partner should question himself or herself, "What do I need?" and "What does my partner require?" and both couples should make it a practice to convey their demands properly. It takes some practice at first, but it can become a habit after a while.

21.) Experiment with New Things Together

Look for something new you can learn or attempt together. This could be a hobby, a pastime, or an adventure. Anything works, as long as neither of you have done it before and can share the excitement of attempting it for the first time together.

22.) Let's Take a Look Back at Our Lives Together

Sit down with a glass of wine or a cup of tea and reflect on your life together. You might look over your old photos and talk about everything you've gone through together through-out your relationship. You can also think of things you would like to do together in the future.

23. The Gratitude List

The Gratitude List is an excellent couple's therapy exercise. It enables each person to rearrange their thoughts about their mate and become aware of all the subtle positive elements that led them to fall in love with each other in the first place.

Jot down at least five qualities you admire or respect in your mate. This might be followed by three things you could do in the relationship to help your partner feel more loved and respected. If you feel ready, you might extend the practice by keeping a daily thankfulness notebook for 2-4 weeks.

This will help you concentrate on the positive aspects of your relationship and become aware of the small positive things they observe about their partner regularly.

24.) The Relationship Check-In

This couple's therapy exercise is beneficial to all relationships. It increases communication between spouses and gives each of them a chance to speak. Set aside 30-60 minutes per week to discuss your most recent experiences, dreams, what you want and need from each other, and how you may strengthen your relationship.

CHAPTER 12: COMMON RELATIONSHIP MISTAKES

Our happiness in life is not entirely dependent on having a close relationship, but it is surely boosted by having healthy and tight bonds. If yours do not seem to be operating as well as you'd like, it is conceivable that some little modifications will get everything back on track.

One of the most rapidly increasing areas of psychology is the study of close relationships and well-being. We know that close connections are beneficial to health, as demonstrated by a recent study from the University of Massachusetts. We now recognize some of the most prevalent obstacles that people experience, thanks to various long-term studies that have monitored successful and unsuccessful couples over time. By detecting problems early on, you can overcome these obstacles before they become insurmountable.

1. Taking your relationship for granted

As relationships mature, it is common to assume that it is acceptable to let the typical niceties of life slip and slide. Some of this is natural, appropriate, and even beneficial to relationships. However, it never hurts to consider what life would be like if you didn't have your partner. What would this entail for your daily life, overall well-being, and thoughts about your future happiness? Once you begin to build an image of yourself apart from your spouse, this image may help you go the additional mile to show your partner affection, interest, and worry, even if just for a little while. It is all too simple to ignore those closest to you because you expect them to be there no matter what. By doing so, they may seek out persons who will offer them the attention they lack from you.

2. Becoming too dependent

People who are nervously attached might become so clingy and dependent on their spouses that they can push them away due to their overwhelming demand for affection and reassurance. After you and your relationship have established your commitment to each other, you should not have to question and wondering whether your partner truly cares constantly. Even if you have not entered the commitment stage, you should be able to detect whether he or she is interested in you based on "behavioral" evidence. Such information could include remembering to contact or text you, being cordial and performing your favors, and being pleasant to the individuals you care about. If not these indicators, there may be others specific to your connection that, if you pay attention, reveal how much he or she cares for you, which should help you feel less apprehensive about the relationship.

3. Allowing your relationship's limits to erode

There are sure to be secrets in any form of close connection. Allowing outsiders into your private life, even if it appears to be completely innocent, might damage your partner's confidence in you and your relationship. If your partner discovers the truth, he or she will feel deceived, if not embarrassed. For example, say you tell a relative that your boyfriend dislikes his boss. Let us also assume that your relative and your partner's boss are unlikely ever to meet. However, there is always the probability of a random chance meeting. Furthermore, what if your relative forgets that this is a secret and brings it up in conversation? Worst-case scenario: what if the secret is revealed on Facebook as a result of someone's oversharing? It will be obvious that you provided the information. Your partner may never find out that you have been snitching, but the fact that you have can put your relationship in peril. You may begin to feel doomed and anxious due to having opened your mouth, emotions that can grow unpleasant and problematic over time.

4. Complaining to everyone about your partner

We can all think of ways to improve our long-term companions. Rather than telling your partner, you may choose to communicate your dissatisfaction with everyone who will listen. But if you do not tell your partner directly what is hurting you, he or she is unlikely to know that you'd like to see some changes in his or her behavior. In addition, by continually focusing on what bothers you, you will find it more difficult to notice the good in your partner. Negative thoughts about your partner's tiny annoyances might build up over time and eventually prevent you from appreciating their desirable and charming features.

5. Activating the passive-aggressive switch

In a close relationship, there are numerous ways to be passive-aggressive. Everything from "ignoring" to do something you'd rather not do to agreeing to a recommendation you never normally follow... the list is nearly limitless. You may believe that it is better not to protest to a request or disagree with anything your partner says aloud, but you cut off a communication channel by not expressing your true feelings. Of course, not all passive-aggressive activities are conscious. For example, you may be neglecting to do your partner a favor, for example, setting the bedroom alarm for an early morning appointment, since you'd rather sleep in than wake up at the crack of dawn. However, it could indicate that you are dissatisfied with why your spouse has to wake up so early, whether it's to catch an early flight or take the ex's children to daycare. Suppose you are exhibiting this type of behavior, and it is not typical of you (for example, you are typically very organized). In that case, you should take some time to focus on what is truly upsetting you and then discuss it openly with your partner.

6. You constantly doubt your connection

Do you ever wonder if you and your partner will still be together in a week, a month, or a year? Are you terrified of jeopardizing your relationship by saying or doing the wrong thing? Do you see your partner's displays of preoccupation as proof of his or her disinterest in you? As previously stated, it is beneficial to take your partner for granted in some ways. However, this is a slightly different take on the subject. When you question your relationship, it suggests you doubt it will last, and, as a result, you may be less likely to feel comfortable making future commitments. If you are continuously looking for a "Plan B," your spouse may pick up on it, and the relationship's doom may become a real possibility.

7. Failing to take your partner seriously

When you consider the most indispensable persons and things of your life, how would you prioritize your partner? Do your children come first in your life? What about your coworkers or your job? It may be extremely logical and understandable to prioritize your children, for example, because they need you. But our romantic relationship has different characteristics to our relationships with our children or other family members (parents, siblings, and so on). There is no need to choose between who is more significant. However, by engaging in this thinking experiment, you can receive insight into how your relationship fits your broader life goals. If there is a significant mental gap between your children, career, friends, or other persons and involvements, it is possible that your partner feels undervalued. If you are at a social gathering, notice whether you dismiss your companion in favor of others, departing at the end of the evening without speaking more than a word or two. Even if your partner does not admit to feeling snubbed, this lack of focus will be perceived as rejection and will detract from your partner's feelings toward you over time.

8. Giving up on your relationship

Everyone has difficulties, whether it is losing a job, dealing with health issues, or overcoming an addiction. At these difficult times, your partner requires your encouragement and support, but it is also during these times that you may be feeling the most anxious. Therefore, it is more crucial than ever at those times to hang in there and allow your spouse to know that he or she will get through this tough moment. Your confidence and support will not only assist in alleviating your spouse's agony but may also be precisely what they need to summon the resources necessary to face the difficulty.

9. A sense of hopelessness

The list of possible causes for feeling hopeless can include infidelity, differences in personalities, habits, and ideals, or simple misunderstandings that escalate into outright hostility. If you permit yourself to give up on the situation, you will be significantly less likely to invest emotionally in the measures necessary for relationship restoration. People acquire despair in their relationships due to a series of cognitive errors, such as believing that what is terrible now will always be awful, that life "should" be worry-free. Catch yourself before these cognitive twists take hold, and you'll be more likely to focus on what is good in your relationship rather than what is terrible.

Numerous elements must be considered when establishing long-term relationships. However, avoiding these typical pitfalls is a fantastic place to start if you want to keep yours healthy for years to come.

CHAPTER 13: RESTORATIVE PRACTICES TO RESOLVE CONFLICT

We all experience conflict in our marriage at one point or another. Restorative practices are a way to resolve the conflict and get back on the right track. In addition, they can help with emotional intelligence and understanding your partner's needs better.

Our world is changing at an unbelievable rate. Globally, social patterns that have long characterized human life are shifting radically. Social links among families, schools, businesses, and communities are deteriorating, but humans are designed to connect. We need good and meaningful connections just as we need food, housing, and clothing to thrive.

What exactly are restorative practices?

Restorative practices are a new social science that investigates ways to improve interpersonal and community interactions. When put into practice, the results can be dramatic.

Students in schools feel more protected and a sense of belonging, which leads to better behavior, less bullying, and less violence. Likewise, leaders in the workplace enable direct contact among employees and address conflict when it emerges. As a result, performance is improved, accountability is increased, and collaboration is more effective.

New choices in criminal justice allow victims and offenders to mend the emotional suffering inflicted by crime. In addition, restorative techniques give ordinary people a stronger voice in the problems that matter most in our communities.

Restorative practices, in a nutshell, are the science of connections and community. Individual daily contacts have a significant impact on the world around you, at work, with young people, and in your community.

Using a restorative approach in education is not a new craze; its roots may be traced back hundreds of years to long-established indigenous groups such as Native Americans, Indigenous Australians, and Maoris. When there was misbehavior or dispute in their community, they would gather in a circle to discuss it respectfully and agree on reparation.

In contrast to traditional, punitive techniques of discipline, which focus on who is to blame and what punishment should be meted out, the restorative approach considers what harm has been done and how it might be repaired. It is founded on the restorative values of empathy, accountability, and making things right for everyone involved. Relationships are key to the restorative approach. Relationships, Responsibility, Reparation, and Resilience are what we call the '4 Rs of a Restorative Approach.'

There are numerous reasons why employing a restorative approach is especially vital in today's environment. For example, we are witnessing an alarming increase in knife crime, a lack of sense of belonging, and an increase in mental health difficulties among young people. Furthermore, the increased usage of digital media reduces our face-to-face connection, implying that youngsters spend less time acquiring social skills such as empathy. Yet, empathy has been shown to influence children's future success in all areas of life, including relationships, professions, and emotional well-being. A restorative approach can help to restore this balance. It not only seeks to repair harm and reestablish relationships, but the process and questions involved give children the confidence to take responsibility for their actions, recognize the impact of their actions on others, develop empathy, appreciate how their thoughts and feelings affect their behavior, and learn important problem-solving skills. All of this increases their resilience and capacity to deal with whatever life throws at them.

All of this contrasts sharply with sanction-based discipline, which typically does not result in long-term behavioral change, but rather can lead to relationship breakdowns and resentment, or simply a change in behavior to avoid punishment, rather than an understanding that it may be wrong or harmful. It also does not provide students the opportunity to learn from their mistakes.

Restorative techniques have the potential to:

- decrease crime, violence, and bullying

- enhance human behavior

- strengthen civil society

- encourage excellent leadership.

- rebuild relationships

- rectify any damage

HOW CAN I APPLY RESTORATIVE TECHNIQUES IN MY HOME?

Recognize and appreciate daily demonstrations of empathy! Encourage relationships with people of various backgrounds (including those who are different from us) by having dialogues about how our positive behaviors and acts of kindness influence others.

When children have difficulty describing their sentiments, encourage them to utilize the phrase "I feel... when... because..." Again, focus on individual views rather than assigning "responsibility" to others.

When harm occurs, ask youngsters to consider the situation from the perspective of another person.

Set aside time as a family to develop a shared strategy for actions inside and outside the home. Discuss how you want your activities to be perceived by the rest of the world. Having a common vision will aid in holding each other accountable.

Encourage children to devise their own solutions for the damage they have created. Encourage them to consider who and how their actions impacted others.

Practice and reward empathic listening during family discussions! For example, "I heard you say...", "I like what you said about...", and "I heard you say, and I think..." go a long way toward showing children that they are heard and cared about.

Restorative Parenting

While restorative language can be used in everyday life — talking about and sharing our ideas and feelings in a supportive, non-judgmental manner – let's look at how it can be used specifically in response to an incident in a normal family scenario:

Assume a disagreement has broken out between siblings due to the younger sister entering her older sister's room and taking something without asking. In a more conventional method, the younger sister might be forced to return it and warned that she must not do it again, that she must respect her sister's property, and that she must ask before using things. Alternatively, the older sister may be advised that she needs to understand her younger sister and share her belongings. Both options may temporarily remedy the dilemma, but do they suit their needs? Is there any learning going on, and what might happen next time?

We want any infraction or "misbehavior" to be used as a teaching tool. After all, the word "discipline" is derived from the root word "disciple," which means "to educate or guide" rather than "to punish". Using a restorative approach accomplishes exactly that.

Using a restorative approach, the parent would bring the two together and ask each of them a series of neutral, non-judgmental questions without assigning blame. They would ask the first youngster what happened, what they were thinking or feeling at the time, and then rephrase what they'd heard before asking the second child the same questions. (Paraphrasing is important because it not only clarifies your understanding of what happened and shows the child that you listened to them, but it also ensures that the other child hears their sibling's side of the story – they may not be listening when their sibling says it, especially if they are angry at them, but they will listen when you do.) Hearing one another's stories and how they felt/are feeling is extremely powerful and helps youngsters develop empathy and see the impact of their actions on others. It has a significantly greater impact than merely being told by an adult. Next, you might ask them whether anyone else has been affected and how; this allows them to recognize the broader consequences of their actions. Then you would ask each person in turn what needs to be done to restore the damage. It is critical that they come up with solutions and that we do not intervene. As adults, we frequently believe that we know what is best and what needs to be done, but we do not always know what the children require to make things better, and you could be surprised at what they come up with. You must agree with both parties on what needs to be done. Therefore, you may need to go back and forth if they do not agree on a solution at first. You can accomplish this simply by asking, 'Can you think of anything else on which you and I can both agree?' Once you have reached an agreement on a course of action, ask, "How can we make sure this doesn't happen again?" Allow them to come up with ideas again and appreciate all of them until they develop one feasible one.

Using a restorative approach returns the conflict to people who must resolve it. It allows the 'victim' to be heard while also allowing the 'harmer' to realize how their actions have affected others and empowering them to make things right.

The relationship is repaired through healing the damage. A restorative approach is a respectful, responsive manner of dealing with the wrongdoing that results in a peaceful, happy household where everyone feels valued and respected, and most importantly, where they feel they belong.

CHAPTER 14: COMMUNICATE BETTER WITH YOUR PARTNER

Focus on how you say things if you want to know how to communicate better with your partner. Dr. John Gottman's study has revealed the components of effective communication between intimate partners.

Do you want to know how to talk to your lover as though you adore them?

What are the components of how we understand our partners when they are attempting to communicate with us?

If you wish to improve your communication with your spouse, read on.

Surprisingly, the research shows that our partner's actual words contribute only 7% of the message, while our partner's pattern of speech and tone of voice contributes over 40%. Thus, words that appear to be innocent on the surface can become cruel when delivered in a dismissive, sarcastic, or contemptuous tone.

We all know that tone of voice is an important part of communication. However, research indicates that other factors such as timbre, volume, tone, and inflection all have a significant effect.

Over two years, researchers from the University of Southern California videotaped hundreds of discussions from marriage counseling sessions. They meticulously examined elements such as volume, pitch, and timbre, paying special attention to how the voice varies during moments of mounting emotion. The researchers were especially drawn to how the speaking spouse's voice influenced the listening partner. The second group of researchers examined changes in emotions such as blame or acceptance as a control.

So how do you improve your communication with your spouse?

Keep an eye on your habitual speech patterns.

"It isn't only a matter of studying your feelings. It is about researching the emotional impact of what your partner says." — Shrikanth Narayanan, USC Professor, and Researcher.

The study found that communication is more about how you express something than what you say. According to this study, habitual voice and speech patterns were a more accurate predictor of marital development than behaviors.

"Psychological practitioners and scholars have long recognized that how partners communicate about and discuss problems has significant implications for the quality of their relationships. The lack of effective and reliable instruments for measuring the crucial parts in those dialogues, on the other hand, has been a major hurdle to their broad clinical application. These findings mark a significant step forward in making objective measurement of behavior realistic and viable for couple therapists," said University of Utah researcher Brian Baucom.

What are the most important elements of how your partner hears you?

A fundamental takeaway from successful science-based couples counseling is to develop mindfulness in what you say and how you say it.

Volume

Yelling is ineffective.

Raising your voice will encourage your partner to respond by shouting back or fleeing. In either case, you are not communicating or bargaining. Instead, try lowering your voice when you speak to your partner. Use silence and pauses to stress what is most important to you while also giving your spouse time to contemplate and respond.

Timbre

Timbre is a term that you may be less familiar with. It is the "color" or emotionality of your voice. Your partner uses timbre to establish a "felt sense" of what you are saying. Begin to notice the timbre (or lack of resonance) of your voice (i.e., angry, frustrated, sad). Learn to be more conscious of how your emotions are communicated through your speaking voice.

Pitch

The pitch of your voice indicates how high or low it sounds. Pitch may often reveal your emotional condition or even how honest you are. A high-pitched voice, for example, may indicate a defensive stance when speaking to your partner. On the other hand, if your vocal tone rises at the end of a remark, it sounds more like an inquiry and indicates to your partner that you are either unsure or fake.

Pace

When you have a dispute with your intimate partner, pay attention to how quickly you are speaking.

Take note of your own vocal pace, especially if it differs from that of your partner. For example, slow down if you tend to speak quicker as you become angrier.

You are both looking for the same thing...to be understood.

Remember that you love your partner and that you both want to be understood better. Often, the best way to accomplish this is to concentrate on helping your spouse "get you." This is generally best accomplished by slowing down.

But do not be too slow

Going too slowly can be perceived as condescending and even scornful. It has an embedded message that says, "I think you are an idiot."

Speak at a steady pace, pause for emphasis, and check-in with your companion to see if they are also maintaining calm.

One of the sad characteristics of modern life is that we place the qualities of respect and politeness in what I like to refer to as a "stranger space." But, unfortunately, courtesy, respect, and civility also apply to your beloved intimate partner.

The ultimate tip to improved communication with your partner...

Address to your partner as if they were a loved one.

These suggestions will assist you in making regular deposits into each other's emotional bank accounts.

Terry Real, one of my favorite couple's therapists, has often said, "Speak to your spouse as if they were someone you care about."

CHAPTER 15: LOVING A PERSON WITH ANXIETY

Having a spouse who suffers from anxiety or has an anxiety disorder can be challenging.

"Spouses may find themselves in roles they do not want to play, such as compromiser, protector, or comforter," writes Kate Thieda, MS, LPCA, NCC, a therapist and author of the excellent book *Loving Someone with Anxiety*.

They may have to shoulder additional obligations and avoid specific places or activities that cause their partner discomfort, she said. This can be quite difficult for couples and their relationships.

"Partners of loved ones suffering from anxiety may become angry, upset, depressed, or disillusioned because their hopes for how the relationship will develop have been thwarted by anxiety."

Thieda's book assists partners in better understanding anxiety and using ways that support their spouses without feeding into or enabling their anxieties.

She outlined five strategies for doing so and what to do if your partner refuses treatment:

1. Become knowledgeable about anxiety.

It is important to know everything about anxiety, including the various types of anxiety disorders and how to treat them. This will allow you to grasp your partner's situation better.

Remember that your companion may not fall into any of these categories. "The bitter truth is, it doesn't matter whether your partner's anxiety is 'diagnosable,'" argues Thieda. However, if it is affecting your relationship or lowering your partner's or your quality of life, it is worthwhile to make changes."

2. Avoid easing your partner's concern.

"Partners frequently end up making accommodations for their partner's anxiety, whether it is intentional, such as playing the superhero, or simply because it makes life easier, such as doing all the chores because their partner is afraid of driving," said Thieda.

Making accommodations, on the other hand, aggravates your partner's anxiousness. For one thing, she claims, it provides your partner with no reason to overcome their anxiety. Second, it gives the message that there is something to be afraid of, which adds to their anxiousness.

3. Establish boundaries.

Your partner may continue to want accommodations, such as having you drive everywhere or stay at their home frequently, according to Thieda. "You have the right to a life, too, and this may entail telling your partner, lovingly, that you will do what you need and want to do."

Thieda spends an entire chapter in her book efficiently explaining this to the partners of anxious personalities. She recommends being compassionate, using "I" expressions, and making clear demands.

She presents the following instances, for example: Instead of saying, "You worry too much about what other people think of you," you may say, "I'm afraid that your anxieties about what other people think of you are causing you to perform poorly at work."

Instead of saying, "Do not call me at work so much," you could add, "It would be great if you would try some of the soothing strategies you have learned before phoning me at the workplace."

She also advises to "always examine whether a compromise is possible, but also acknowledge that you have the freedom to do things independently."

4. Unwind as a group.

There are numerous strategies you can try jointly to reduce anxiety. "The body scan is an excellent couples mindfulness practice because one person can help the other through the process," Thieda says.

According to her, the spouse delivering instructions must pay attention to timing as well as exact directions. She also stated that the partner receiving the instructions must pay attention to each body part and release its tension. This encourages mindfulness in both couples.

5. Concentrate on your well-being.

"When you live with an anxious spouse, there can be a lot of tension in your relationship and your home," Thieda writes in her book. Having self-care practices and goals in place can assist you in dispelling the static.

Consider what you are already doing to enhance physical, spiritual, mental, emotional, professional, and relational wellness. Assessing your current situation allows you to better grasp where you need to go. For example, you might want to make goals for bettering your health or seek help from others. In addition, you might wish to see a therapist or join a support group.

What Should You Do If Your Partner Refuses Treatment?

Anxiety is a highly treatable condition. However, your partner may be unwilling to seek expert assistance. Thieda urges that they evaluate the grounds behind their refusal.

One reason treatment "fails" is that it is not the correct remedy for anxiety. For example, they may have tried therapy in the past, but it did not work. "It is better to work with a professional who uses cognitive behavioral therapy techniques and is specifically trained in working with those who battle with anxiety," Thieda advises.

They could have attempted medication or psychotherapy independently, but she believes a combination of treatments would be more effective. It is also possible that your spouse tried to take on too much and became even more worried as a result. "Perhaps they could take a new approach to their treatment, breaking down the obstacles into smaller, more manageable pieces."

According to Thieda, the decision to seek treatment ultimately rests with your partner. "No amount of begging, pleading, or threatening will be effective and will almost certainly make matters worse."

When they decide to seek assistance, the best thing you can do is be supportive, encouraging, and kind, she says.

Having a spouse who suffers from anxiety may be extremely stressful. You can benefit your partner and your relationship by educating yourself, setting appropriate boundaries, and practicing self-care.

CHAPTER 16: TEN SURPRISING KEYS TO BUILDING A HEALTHY RELATIONSHIP

The 10 keys to a strong relationship are a list of the ingredients required for a satisfying, long-lasting bond.

Your work performance evaluation arrives, and it is shining. There is, however, one area that "requires work." Which part do you remember days later? The negatives, of course. Part of you understands it is foolish to be bothered by just one item. After all, there's a lot more good than bad in there, yet you can't seem to stop yourself from fixating on your mistakes.

Regrettably, we do the same in our love relationships. We all have a predisposition to focus on the negative parts of our experiences. As a result, we are more critical of our connection than we should be. We take the good times for granted, and they become an underappreciated aspect of our partnership.

But what about the issues? They are noticeable. Our partner's insensitive statements, mood swings, and sloppiness frequently hold our focus.

When you combine this with a relationship that has lost some of its luster, it can be hard to think of anything other than the problems. As Daniel Kahneman describes in his book *Thinking, Fast and Slow,* we tend to notice only what is in front of us and ignore what is not. When issues are all you see, it is easy to believe that's all your relationship is.

We have such a strong tendency to focus on the negative that we may create problems that do not exist. According to a study published in *Science,* if our relationship doesn't have any major concerns, we're more likely to view what was earlier considered a minor issue as more serious.

We do not have time to comprehend what is going right when we waste our time worrying about the wrong things. This not only implies that our perception of the relationship is warped, but it also implies that we are passing up an important opportunity. Therefore, while working on problems is one approach to improve a long-term relationship, it is vital to dwell on your partner's strong attributes and the positive aspects of your relationship.

The foundations of healthy partnerships

Begin by paying greater attention to the aspects of your relationship that are steady, consistent, and comfortable. Those tranquil, drama-free parts of the status quo are easy to overlook, but they are sources of power.

The following are ten important pillars of healthy relationships that research says are essential for a pleasant, long-lasting bond. Many of these are probably present in your relationship; all you have to do is pause and pay attention.

1. You are free to be yourself.

You and your spouse accept each other as they are; you do not try to change each other. As a result, you may be yourself and reveal your actual identity without fear of being judged by your companion. This is beneficial since studies suggest that couples who accept each other are more content with their relationships.

2. You are best friends.

Your love partner is your best friend in many respects, and you are theirs. That is excellent news because studies show that romantic couples who emphasize friendship are more committed and have more sexual enjoyment. In addition, friendship-centered romantic partnerships stress emotional support, intimacy, affection, and the maintenance of a solid bond. They also prioritize addressing requirements for caregiving, security, and companionship.

3. You feel at ease and close.

It is not always easy to get close to someone. However, in your partnership, you have worked over it and are now fairly comfortable sharing feelings, leaning on each other, and being emotionally intimate. Even though vulnerability can be difficult at times, you have learned to trust your partner and find that it brings you closer together. You no longer erect emotional barriers and are not always concerned about your partner's departure, which creates a sense of stability.

4. You are more alike than you are different.

You and your partner have a lot in common, and principal areas of similarity may make your relationship more enjoyable. Sure, the distinctions stick out, but you are similar in many respects beyond those few variances. For example, your partner may prefer superhero films while you prefer rom-com. However, you are both homebodies who like cooking a meal together before collapsing on the couch to watch a TV series in which you make fun of poor language and predict the next plot twist. You have far more in common than you do differences.

5. You have a sense of belonging.

Words are important. Do you frequently use terms like "we," "us," and "our" when you speak? For example, do you respond to the question, "What is your favorite show to binge-watch?" with, "We have begun watching *Schitt's Creek*"? Your use of the word "we" demonstrates a strong sense of cognitive proximity, or shared identity, in your connection. According to research, couples that are bonded in this way are more satisfied and committed.

6. They help you become a better person.

Your companion assists you in refining and improving who you are. In this situation, your partner does not take over and tell you how to change but rather supports your self-growth choices. You seek fresh and intriguing experiences that add to a sense of self-development as a group. According to relationship experts, when you extend and grow as a person, your relationship expands and grows as well.

7. You have a portion of the authority.

While partners may have different areas of skill (for example, one may manage lawn maintenance while the other handles interior decoration), couples frequently share decision-making, control, and influence in the relationship. Relationships are stronger, more satisfying, and more likely to last when both partners have a say. In addition, couples are happier, predictably, when they believe the division of labor in their relationship is equitable.

8. You share positive characteristics

What characteristics do people look for in a spouse? It is shockingly straightforward: dependability, warmth, kindness, fairness, trustworthiness, and intellect. Though these characteristics are not spectacular and may not immediately spring to mind when making a wish list for your mate, they lay the groundwork for a strong relationship. According to research, partners who have amiable and emotionally stable personalities are more fulfilled in their relationship.

9. You have mutual trust.

We must be able to count on our partners, which stems from trust. We do not just trust our spouse with our phone passwords or access to our bank accounts; we also know that our partner always has our best interests in mind and will be there for us when we need them the most. According to research, this is a positive cycle: trust fosters deeper commitment, encouraging even more trust.

10. You do not have any major problems.

There are issues, and then there are major problems. Relationship killers include "dark side" concerns such as contempt, infidelity, jealously, and emotional or physical violence. Light can sometimes originate from the absence of darkness.

Spend some time thinking about how each of these applies to your relationship. You might wish to assign yourself a score at this stage to confirm that your relationship is in good health. How many of the ten pillars do you possess? How many are you missing? The objective is to increase our ability to notice and cultivate these core areas. Strengthening these pillars is often as simple as relishing everything that works in your relationship. When you know what to look for, you can find a lot.

Hopefully, you have also identified areas of strength that are not listed here. That is fantastic because this list is far from exhaustive. More importantly, it reveals that you are noticing more of what works rather than dwelling on what is broken.

Of course, a few benefits should not be used to excuse staying in a terrible relationship. Focusing on one's strengths is only beneficial for individuals who want to improve their relationships. Mutual respect, love, and friendship amongst equals are the foundations of good partnerships.

The lesson here is also not to pretend that your relationship is without flaws. Rather, it is much easier to resolve such issues when you recognize how much of your relationship is currently working well. Relationships are difficult enough without adding to the difficulty. When you are simply pointing out what is wrong, it is easy to fall prey to the incorrect notion that your relationship is in peril. However, if you stop taking the good for granted and start giving your spouse and relationship more credit, you may discover that your relationship is stronger than you believe.

CONCLUSION

Anxiety can cause difficulties in all aspects of your life, including your romantic relationships. Is your relationship being strained by anxiety?

You can take practical efforts to reduce your anxiety and feel more relaxed and secure. Your most critical connections will benefit as you minimize your worry.

When we become nervous, our bodies respond with an increased stress reaction. Our heart rate, breathing rate, and stress hormones all increase. When we are experiencing personal difficulty, most individuals turn to their companions. What happens next is influenced by our partner's reply. We feel reassured and soothed when someone we trust reacts with support. As a result, our body relaxes and returns to a condition of balance and serenity.

When one member of a partnership suffers from an anxiety problem, they require extra assistance and may be more difficult to soothe. This might put pressure on the unaffected partner and cause a great deal of distress. If the unaffected partner feels stressed, he or she may need to learn how to create healthy limits.

Adults with anxiety have higher degrees of suffering in relationships, according to research. When one partner experiences significant anxiety and suffering, the unaffected partner is likewise severely troubled.

When you or your partner suffers from chronic anxiety, it can put a strain on your relationship. Anxiety can drive the affected partner to refuse to participate in family or social activities, isolating both of you. Anxiety can also lead to difficulties in the workplace, causing financial hardship on top of other challenges such as diminished well-being. Therefore, it is critical to monitor your stress levels and check-in with your partner.

The contrast between fear and anxiety is an important yet contentious one in anxiety and stress disorders. Fear and anxiety share many similarities in terms of psychological, behavioral, physiological, and neurological aspects. However, there are some significant differences between the two. Fear is commonly defined as a phasic and rapid fight-or-flight response followed by acute arousal in response to a specific and imminent threat. On the other hand, anxiety is frequently described as a longer protracted feeling of tension, concern, and apprehension over unclear and potentially unpleasant future events. Although both fear and anxiety play crucial evolutionary roles in keeping us safe, fear allows us to combat or escape immediate threats or danger. In contrast, anxiety heightens alertness and improves our capacity to discern unknown impending risks. However, anxiety disorders can arise when the anxiety or dread response is excessive or happens in the absence of an actual threat, either immediate or future.

Anxiety can affect how we behave in the relationship in two distinct (and contradictory) ways. First, anxiety might cause us to become overly reliant or extremely avoidant.

When we are nervous and uncertain, we may rely too heavily on our partner to help us cope with our anxiety. We may also experience feelings of insecurity and envy, which can lead to unfounded suspicions or paranoia. Constant reassurance is required in this situation.

Anxiety might also cause us to distance ourselves from others, forcing us to avoid becoming too close to them. We may want to keep our independence because it feels safer. We are protected from getting hurt or disappointed when we avoid emotional closeness. Maintaining a sense of separation from others, even when we seek connection, can make a healthy relationship with our partner challenging.

It is critical to recognize that anxiety disorders are highly curable. Whether general or specialized, therapy for anxiety disorders is frequently helpful and can bring significant relief from distress.

Cognitive Behavior Therapy (CBT) teaches you how to identify and examine harmful thought processes. CBT is frequently beneficial in the treatment of both anxiety and mood disorders. (Many persons who suffer from anxiety also suffer from depression.)

Seek assistance. Our relationships flourish when we feel more at ease and safe in ourselves. If you or your relationship is suffering from anxiety, you must seek therapy and get yourself and your partner back on track with better connection and emotional confidence.

LOVE YOURSELF AND TAKE CARE OF YOUR LOVED ONES.